LITTLE TALKS WITH GOD

LITTLE TALKS
WITH GOD

Catherine of Siena

Edited and Mildly Modernized by
HENRY L. CARRIGAN, JR.

PARACLETE PRESS
BREWSTER, MASSACHUSETTS

Library of Congress Cataloging-in-Publication Data

Catherine, of Siena, Saint, 1347–1380.
   Little talks with God / Catherine of Siena ; edited and mildly
modernized by Henry L. Carrigan, Jr.
      p. cm.
   Includes bibliographical references.
    ISBN 1-55725-272-6 (pbk.)
     1. Catherine, of Siena, Saint, 1347–1380. 2. Christian women
saints–Italy–Biography. 3. Spiritual life–Catholic Church.
I. Carrigan, Henry L., 1954– II. Title.
   BX4700.C4 A3 2001
   248.4'82–dc21

                                                  00-012922

2001 First Printing
2004 Second Printing
2006 Third Printing
© 2001 by Paraclete Press
ISBN 1-55725-272-6

10 9 8 7 6 5 4 3

Published by Paraclete Press
Brewster, Massachusetts
www.paracletepress.com

Printed in the United States of America.

CONTENTS

INTRODUCTION

On October 4, 1970, the Roman Catholic Church awarded the title of doctor of the church to two women: Teresa of Avila and Catherine of Siena. The writings and teachings of both these women remain very popular today, but it is Catherine's writings that teach us the most about incorporating our spiritual natures and our quests for union with God into our daily lives.

Although she is often called a mystic like Meister Eckhart, Catherine combined her own mystical experiences with a fervent activism. She was a Dominican, but she was not a cloistered member of that Order. Instead, from the very beginning she was active in ministering to the sick and aiding the poor. She also played a significant role in the politics of church and state in fourteenth-century Italy. Yet, in the midst of her activism, Catherine's quest for justice and equity was founded in her own experience of union with God. The knowledge and truth that she gained from this encounter strengthened her, as she worked tirelessly to share God's love and compassion with those around her.

Catherine reached out to her society by writing her works in the language of the people rather than in the Latin of the Church. So popular were her books that they were some of the first to be brought into print. She had a devoted and large following among all classes of society in Siena, and they considered her their teacher.

Catherine was a prolific letter writer, but it is *The Dialogue*, titled *Little Talks with God* in this edition, that has brought her teachings to the widest audience. In it she offers a glimpse of the means whereby God's grace and mercy may be known in full knowledge and truth. *Little Talks with God* provides spiritual seekers a guidebook for incorporating the spiritual into the mundane.

Biography

Biographers of Catherine have faced great difficulties in reconstructing the life of their subject, because her life is so embedded in legend and piety. In addition, some of the earliest biographies of Catherine were themselves hagiographies, creating a portrait of a pious mystical woman whose transports to God made her an unreachable subject. Even so, there are many facets of Catherine's life of which we can be sure.

Catherine was born in 1347 to a wool dyer in the Fontebranda district of Siena. Caterina di Giacomo di Benincasa, a precocious young girl, was the twenty-fourth of twenty-five children. She was a headstrong and independent child, clever and ingenious in her religious devotion. Catherine's passionate desire for truth and the knowledge of God motivated her very being, even in her youth.

The Dominican Order influenced Catherine greatly. She often visited the church and cloister of San Domenico, a hub of Dominican teaching, spending a great deal of time with these teachers. She was also influenced in Dominican teachings by the brother of her brother-in-law, Tommaso della Fonte, who had joined the Dominican order in 1349.

Another group that impressed Catherine was a group of women in Siena known as the *Mantellate*. These women, who wore the habit of the Dominican Order, lived in their homes and ministered to the sick and poor. Even though they did not live in a cloister, they were directed by a prioress. By the time she was fourteen, Catherine had decided not to marry, and she sought and gained entrance to this group of women.

Raymond Capua, her earliest biographer and close friend, records that Catherine vowed her virginity to God when she was just seven years old. At fifteen, she defied her parents and refused their efforts to force her to marry, and at eighteen she obtained the Dominican habit. After she joined the Dominicans, she lived for a period of about three years in silence and solitude, leaving her room only to attend Mass. By the time she was twenty-one, she had experienced her "mystical espousal" to Christ. Soon after she began her work with the *Mantellate*.

Much like Mother Teresa, Catherine devoted herself to taking care of the sick and indigent. However, during this period of ministering to society, she never gave up her contemplative life, and could often be found at home in her room teaching her followers about the Bible, theology, and God's grace and truth.

In 1370, Catherine had one of her most profound mystical experiences—her "mystical death." For four hours she experienced ecstatic union with God, even though to outside observers she appeared to be dead. This experience led her to become more severe in her self-discipline, and enabled her to have a clear vision of the ways that she could introduce God's truth to the world.

From the time of her "mystical death" to her physical death, Catherine worked tirelessly in political and religious affairs. In 1375, in Pisa, she preached that military strength could be best used to win unbelievers in the Holy Land. She preached that shedding one's blood for Christ was an honorable mission, and so she supported a Crusade through her words. In the same year she received the stigmata, though by her own request these wounds were not visible.

Catherine soon became involved in urging Gregory XI to move the papacy from Avignon back to Rome. During these years she was also active in preaching about clergy reform and martyrdom through Crusades. After Gregory's death, Urban VI replaced him as pope. Because many people opposed Urban when he was elected pope, Catherine foresaw the possibility that schism could occur in the Church. She began a furious letter-writing campaign in order to urge fidelity to the Church. Much of this urging makes its way into her book, *The Dialogue.*

Sometime between 1375 and 1378, Catherine founded a women's monastery outside of Siena in the old fortress of Belcaro. During these years she wrote *The Dialogue.* In this, her most famous writing, she expressed many of her concerns about Church unity, personal austerity and devotion, love of neighbor, clergy reform, God's grace and mercy, and the passionate search for God's truth.

From the time Catherine was thirty until her death at thirty-three, she directed a "household" in Siena where women and men lived by strict observance to poverty and alms. Her final years were filled with physical agony, even though she managed to attend services at Saint Peter's each day. She died on April 29, 1380, and since 1969, the Roman Catholic Church has observed this day as her Feast day.

The Dialogue

Although there is some controversy about whether Catherine wrote this, her most famous work, or dictated it, there is no question that its genesis is in some powerful ecstatic experience. Her friend Raymond of Capua writes:

> So about two years before her death, such a clarity of Truth was revealed to her from heaven that Catherine was constrained to spread it abroad by means of writing, asking her secretaries to stand ready to take down whatever came from her mouth as soon as they noticed that she had gone into ecstasy. Thus in a short time was composed a certain book that contains a dialogue between a soul who asks the Lord four questions, and the Lord himself, who replies to the soul, enlightening her with many useful truths.

In another passage Raymond notes, "When peace had been proclaimed, she returned home and attended more diligently to the composition of a certain book, which she dictated in her own dialect, inspired by the supernal Spirit."

The structure of the book itself derives from Catherine's own concerns about the nature of truth and the unity of the Church. *The Dialogue* opens with her four prayers to God: for herself, for the reform of the Church, for the whole world and for those causing schism in the Church, and for a particular unnamed sinner. Each portion of Catherine's little talks with God reveals God's answers to these four prayers.

Above all, these talks involve Catherine's own restless search for the truth that is God. According to *The Dialogue*, our ecstatic union with God teaches us the humility we need in order to know God as Truth and Love. Out of God's great love, we are enabled to love our neighbors with the love that God has for us. Nowhere is this better expressed than in the opening paragraph of these "little talks":

> When the soul is lifted by a great, yearning desire for the honor of God and the salvation of souls, it practices the ordinary virtues and remains in the cell of self-knowledge, so that it may know better God's goodness toward it. It does this because knowledge must come before love, and only when it has attained love can it strive to follow and to clothe itself with the truth.

And loving, she seeks to pursue truth and clothe herself in it. Catherine's "little talks" provide us with a means whereby we can fold our own eager quest for God's love and truth into the many and busy pathways of our daily lives.

A Word about the Text

I have used Algar Thorold's translation of *The Dialogue*. Thorold's translation was first published in 1907 by Kegan Paul, Trench, Trubner & Co. Ltd. London.

To make the text more relevant for today, I have abridged it considerably. I have not included many portions of *The Dialogue* that pertain to Catherine's religious community and the rules that govern it. The material in this edition focuses on how to live the spiritual life.

I have remained true to the spirit of the text, even where I have mildly modernized it. Mostly, my modernizations have come in three areas. First, I have replaced archaic words and forms of address with more modern ones. Thus, "thou" and its related pronoun forms become "you" and its related forms, throughout. Second, I have attempted to use inclusive language in this edition, but I have retained the masculine pronouns for God so as not to be anachronistic. Finally, I have altered Catherine's syntax and sentence structure to make it livelier and more appealing to a contemporary audience. Most often this simply means casting sentences in the active rather than the passive voice.

I am grateful to Robert Edmonson, Buzz Elmer, and Rebecca Howell for their close readings and astute suggestions. This edition is much improved because of their gracious efforts.

I hope that Catherine's words will speak to you even as they spoke to her followers and to the Church over 500 years ago.

Henry L. Carrigan, Jr.
Lancaster, Pennsylvania
The Feast of St. Augustine

A TREATISE OF
DIVINE PROVIDENCE

*How a servant of God, elevated by her desire for
God's honor and for the salvation of her neighbors,
after she had seen the union of the soul with
God, exerted herself in humble prayer and
asked of God four requests.*

When the soul is lifted by a great, yearning
desire for the honor of God and the salvation
of souls, it practices the ordinary virtues and
remains in the cell of self-knowledge, so that it may
know better God's goodness toward it. It does this
because knowledge must come before love, and only
when it has attained love can it strive to follow and
to clothe itself with the truth.

But humble and continuous prayer, founded on
knowledge of oneself and of God, is the best way for
the creature to receive such a taste of the truth.
Following the footprints of Christ crucified, and
through humble and unceasing prayer, the soul is
united with God. He remakes it in his image through
desire, affection, and union of love. Christ seems to

have meant this when he said: Those who keep my commandments are the ones who love me, and I will reveal myself to them; they shall be one with me and I one with them. In several places we find similar words, by which we can see that the soul becomes another Himself through the effect of love.

So you may see this more clearly, I will mention a story that a servant of God told me. When she was exalted in prayer, God did not conceal from her the love that he has for his servants. Instead, he revealed that love, saying to her, "Open the eye of your intellect and gaze into me, and you shall see the beauty of my rational creature. Look at those creatures whom I have created in my image and likeness, and have clothed with the wedding garment of love and adorned with many virtues, by which they are united with me through love. Yet if you should ask me who these are, I should reply," said the gentle and loving Word of God, "they are another me, for they have lost and denied their own will, and they are clothed, united, and conformed to my will." It is therefore true that the soul is united with God through love's affection.

So this servant of God, who wanted to know and follow the truth more faithfully, addressed four requests to the supreme and eternal Father. First, she prayed for herself, for this servant believed that she could not be an example to her neighbor in matters of doctrine and prayer if she did not first obtain her own virtue. Her second prayer was for the reformation of the holy church. The third was a general prayer for the entire world, particularly for the peace of Christians who rebel against and persecute the holy church. In the fourth prayer she asked for divine providence to sustain the world, and to be active in a certain case with which she was concerned.

How this servant's desire grew when God showed her the world's need.

This servant's desire was great and continuous, but it grew even greater when the eternal Truth showed her the world's neediness and its tempestuous offenses against God.

She understood this matter even better from a letter she received from her spiritual father, in which he explained to her the pain and sadness caused by such offenses against God, the loss of soul, and the persecutions against the holy church. This knowledge inflamed her holy desire with grief over offenses against God. She anticipated joyously that God would provide against such great evils. She looked forward to morning's arrival in order to hear Mass. In such communion, the soul binds itself firmly to God, and knows better his truth, since the soul is then in God and God in the soul.

When the hour of Mass arrived in the morning— it was the feast day of Mary—she anxiously sought her usual place. From a deep knowledge of herself and with a feeling of holy justice, she was ashamed of her own imperfection, for it seemed to be the cause of all the world's evils. In this knowledge, she cleansed the stains covering her guilty soul, saying: "Eternal Father, I accuse myself before you, so that you may punish me for my sins in this life. Since my sins cause my neighbor to suffer, I beg you, in your mercy, to punish me for them."

How finite works are insufficient for punishment or requital without love's enduring affection.

Then, the eternal Truth seized her desire and drew it more strongly to himself. Just as in the Old Testament, when a sacrifice was offered to God, a fire came down and drew to him the sacrifice that was acceptable to him, so the pure Truth did to that servant's. He sent down the Holy Spirit's merciful fire and seized the sacrifice of desire that she made of herself, saying: "Dear daughter, do you not know that all the sufferings the soul endures, or can endure, in this life are insufficient to punish even the smallest fault? The offense done to me, the infinite Good, calls for an infinite compensation. Yet, not all the sufferings in this life are punishments; they are given in order to correct and chastise a person's offenses.

"However, the infinite desire of the soul and true contrition, not the endurance of finite pain, can absolve both the guilt and the penalty. For God, who is infinite, desires infinite love and infinite grief. I seek infinite grief from you in two ways: One is through sorrow for your own sins that you have committed against me, your creator; the other is through your sorrow for the sins you see your neighbors commit against me. But those who have infinite desire and grieve when they offend me, or see me offended, are infinitely worthy. And their sufferings, whether spiritual or bodily, compensate for their guilt that deserves an infinite penalty. Even though their works are finite and done in finite time, as long as they possess infinite desire, sustain their suffering with contrition, and express infinite displeasure with their guilt, their pain is worthy.

"The glorious apostle Paul shows that finite works are not satisfactory, either as punishment or compensation, without love's affection. He says: 'If I had the tongues of angels, or could prophesy, or even gave up my body to be burned, if I were without love, these works would do me no good whatever.'"

How desire and contrition of heart compensate,
both for the guilt and the penalty in oneself
and in others; how sometimes they compensate for
the guilt only, and not the penalty.

"Dearest daughter, I have shown you that guilt is not punished in this finite time simply by suffering itself. The pain that the soul endures through the desire, love, and contrition of the heart punishes the guilt, not because of the pain itself, but because of the soul's desire. Every virtue, including desire, has its own life through the crucified Christ, since the soul draws its love from him and faithfully follows his footsteps. Only through the pure and intimate love gained in knowing my goodness, and in the bitterness and contrition of heart gained by self-knowledge, do virtues possess value and do sufferings compensate for the fault. Such knowledge produces in the soul hatred and disapproval of sin and the soul's own sensuality. Through this knowledge, it judges itself worthy of sufferings and unworthy of reward."

The sweet Truth continued: "Notice how such souls, through true repentance, true love, true patience, and true humility, judging themselves worthy of pain and unworthy of reward, endure the patient humility that comprises the above-mentioned recompense. You ask me for sufferings, so that I am compensated for the offenses that my creatures commit against me. You also pray for the will to know and love me, the supreme Truth. Yet, if you want to know and enjoy the eternal Truth perfectly, you should never abandon knowledge of yourself. For by humbling yourself in the valley of humility, you will know me and yourself. From this knowledge you will draw all that you need.

"No virtue has life in itself, except through love, and through humility, which nurses and nurtures charity. Humility will come through self-knowledge, for you will learn that even your own existence comes from me. I have loved both you and others who lived before you were in existence. Through my inexpressible love for you, I willed to create you anew in grace. In the blood of my only-begotten Son, poured out with such a great fire of love, I have washed you and made you a new creature.

"This blood teaches the knowledge of the truth that comes when self-knowledge melts away self-love. In this knowledge of me the soul arouses itself with an inexpressible love, for which it endures constant pain. However, this pain does not afflict or shrink the soul. Instead, it enlarges the soul. Since the soul has known my truth, as well as its own faults and humanity's ingratitude, it endures intolerable suffering, grieving because it loves me. For if it did not love me, it would not suffer so.

"Therefore, you and my other servants who have learned truth in this way, will endure and suffer many trials, injuries, and insults for my name's praise and glory. Carry yourselves, then, with true patience, with true repentance for your sins, and with love of virtue for the glory and praise of my name. If you act in this way, I will forgive your sins and those of my other servants, for the pains you will endure will be sufficient, through the virtue of love, for forgiveness and reward, both in you and in others.

"You yourself will receive the fruit of life when the stains of your ignorance are washed away, and I will forget that you ever offended me. I will forgive others because of the love and affection I feel for you. I will give to them according to the attitude with which they receive my gifts.

"To those who receive humbly the doctrine of my servants, I will grant pardon for their guilt and will remove its penalty, since they will come to true knowledge and sorrow for their sins. Through prayer and their desire to serve me, they will receive the fruit of grace, in greater or lesser degrees, according to the extent that they exercise virtue and grace in general. Because of your desires, they will receive forgiveness of their sins. Be sure, though, that they are not so obstinate in their despair that they condemn the Blood that has so sweetly restored them.

"What fruit do they receive? The fruit I have ordained for them is light. I awake in them the hound of conscience. I make them smell the odor of virtue, and make them delight in my servants' conversations.

"Sometimes I let the world show them its diverse passions, so they will know how unstable the world's passions are, and may lift their desires beyond the world and seek their native country, which is eternal life. I use this, and many other ways you cannot see, to lead them back to grace, so that in them my truth can be fulfilled. I do this because I love them so deeply, for I created them out of my measureless love. I do this also because of my servants' love, desire, and grief, for I accept their tears, sweat, and humble prayers. I am the One who gives them this love for the good of souls, and grief for their loss.

"In general, though, I do not pardon the *punishment* due to them; I forgive only their guilt, since they are not disposed to receive my love or my servants' love with perfect love. They do not grieve bitterly over their sins, nor do they display perfect remorse for the sins they have committed, so they are not pardoned from the punishment, but only from their guilt. Complete forgiveness requires the proper attitude from both giver and receiver. Thus, since they are imperfect, they receive imperfectly the virtues of those who offer them to me, for the sake of sinners in suffering. Because of the light of their conscience, these flawed ones do receive forgiveness for their guilt. And when they begin to learn, they pour forth the corruption of their sins, and thus receive the gift of grace.

"These people are in a state of ordinary understanding. If they have trouble, they receive it as a means of correction. They do not resist too much the patience and compassion of the Holy Spirit, but coming out of their sin, they receive the life of grace. If they are foolish and ignore me and my servant's labors, those things given to them through mercy turn to their own judgment and ruin. This is not a defect of mercy, or of the one who asked mercy for the ungrateful one, but it is due to the person's own hardness of heart. With the hands of his own free will, he has covered his heart with a diamond that, if the Blood does not break it, cannot be broken.

"In spite of this hardness of heart, he can use his free will, while he has time, to pray for my Son's blood. Let him with his own hand apply this blood to the diamond over his heart and shatter it. He will then receive the imprint of that blood that has been shed for him. If the person delays, though, he has no remedy, because he has not used the dowry that I gave him. I gave him memory, to remember my benefits; intellect, to see and know the truth; and affection, so he should love me, the eternal Truth, whom he would have known through the use of his intellect.

"I have given this dowry to you all, and it should return fruit to me, the Father. If someone sells it to the devil, the devil has every right to seize everything that that person has acquired in this life. Filling his memory with the delights of sin and with the recollection of shameful pride, greed, self-love, hatred, and unkindness to his neighbors, his intellect is obscured by his unruly will. Such people as these will receive eternal pain, for they have not repented truly of their sins with regret and displeasure for their guilt.

"You now understand how suffering assuages guilt by perfect remorse, not by finite pain. Those who are perfectly repentant receive not only forgiveness for their guilt, but also pardon from their punishment. If they abandon mortal sin and receive grace, but are not sufficiently remorseful and loving to receive pardon for the punishment also, they go through the pains of Purgatory, which is the second and last means of forgiveness.

"Forgiveness comes, then, through the soul's desire to be united to me, the infinite Good, according to the measure of love attained by the recipient's desire and prayer. A person receives as much of my goodness as he gives to me.

"Work, therefore, to increase the fire of your desire. Do not let a moment pass without crying to me in humility, or without continual prayers to me for your neighbors. I say this to you and your confessor, whom I have given you on earth. Have courage and make yourselves dead to all your own sensuality."

How very pleasing to God is the willing desire to suffer for him.

"The willing desire to bear every pain, even death, for the salvation of souls is very pleasing to me. The more the soul endures, the more it shows that it loves me. By loving me, it comes to know more of my truth. The more it knows, the more pain and intolerable grief it feels at the sins committed by others against me.

"You asked me to sustain you and to punish the faults of others in you. You did not say that you were really asking for love, light, and knowledge of the truth. I have already told you that as love increases, so do grief and pain. Those of you who grow in love also grow in sadness. I say to you all, if you ask, I will give it to you, for I do not deny anything to the one who asks of me in truth.

"The love of divine charity is so closely joined in the soul with perfect patience that neither can leave the soul without the other. If the soul chooses to love me, it should choose also to endure pains for me in whatever way that I send them. Patience cannot be proved in any way other than suffering, and patience is united with love.

"Have courage, for, unless you do, you will not prove yourselves to be spouses of my Truth, and faithful children, nor of the company of those who relish the taste of my honor and the salvation of souls."

How every virtue and every defect is
obtained by means of our neighbor.

"You achieve every virtue and every defect by means of your neighbor. Those who hate me, therefore, injure their neighbor and therefore themselves, who are their own chief neighbors. This injury is both general and particular. It is general, because you are obliged to love your neighbor as yourself. Because you love your neighbor, you should help him spiritually, through prayer and by counseling him with words. Assist him spiritually and temporally with your good will, according to his needs.

"A person who does not love does not help his neighbor, and thus harms himself. He cuts himself off from grace, and harms his neighbor by depriving him of the benefit of the prayers and sweet desires he is bound to offer to me for his neighbor. Every act of help he performs should proceed from the compassion he has because of his love for me.

"Every evil is also done by means of your neighbor. If you do not love me, you cannot have compassion for your neighbor. Thus, all evils derive from the soul's lack of love for me and its neighbor. Since this person does no good, it follows that he must do evil.

"Against whom does he commit evil? First to himself and then to his neighbor. But not against me, for no evil can touch me, except insofar as I count that evil he does to himself as evil done to me. He harms himself through sin, which deprives the neighbor of grace. He hurts his neighbor by not paying him the debt of love that he owes his neighbor. He ought to help his neighbor through the prayer and holy desire he offers to me on the neighbor's behalf.

"This assistance is owed to every rational creature. But such help is more useful when it is offered to those close at hand. You are all compelled to help one another by word, doctrine, good works, and in other respects in which your neighbor may be in need. You should counsel your neighbor exactly as you would counsel yourselves, without any self-love. The person who does not love God does not do this because he has no love toward his neighbor. By not loving God, he does the neighbor a special harm. He does the neighbor evil, not just by not doing the good he might do him, but by doing him positive harm.

"In this way, sin causes a physical and mental injustice. The mental injustice happens as soon as the sinner enjoys the idea of sin, hates virtue, and takes pleasure in sensual self-love, which deprives him of the affection of love that he should have toward me and his neighbor. He then commits one sin after another against his neighbor, according to the various ways that please his perverse, sensual will. Sometimes he engages in cruelty.

"It is general cruelty to see oneself and other creatures in danger of death and damnation, and to do nothing because of lack of grace. The sinner is so cruel that he does not help himself or others by loving virtue and hating vice. He might even want to be crueler by playing the devil and tempting others to forsake virtue and embrace vice. This is spiritual cruelty, for he makes himself the instrument of destroying life and dealing out death.

"Bodily cruelty originates in greed. This cruelty not only hampers a person from helping his neighbor, but also causes him to seize things that belong to others. Sometimes he does this by the arbitrary use of power. Other times he accomplishes it through cheating and fraud. He often forces his neighbor to recover his own goods, and sometimes his own body.

"This miserable vice of cruelty will eventually deprive the one who practices it of all my mercy, unless he practices kindness and compassion toward his neighbor! Sometimes he produces insults, and murder often follows them. He often defiles others and becomes a stinking beast, poisoning not only one or two, but everyone who approaches in love or fellowship.

"If a proud person holds a position of authority, he also produces injustice and cruelty. Whom does pride hurt? Your neighbors. You injure them when, in your opinion of yourself, you make yourself superior to them and look down on them.

"Dearest daughter, grieve over offenses committed against me, and weep over these dead ones, so that, by prayer, the bands of their death may be loosened! Notice how in every kind of person and in every society, sin is always committed against one's neighbor, for there is no sin that does not touch others. You commit a secret sin when you deny your neighbor the things you should give him. You commit an open sin when you perform positive acts of sin.

"It is thus true that every sin committed against me is done by means of your neighbors."

How our relationships with our neighbors
lead us to virtue, and why it is that
virtues differ in every person.

"I have told you how negative relationships with our neighbors lead to all sins, because we deprive people of the respect of love, which gives light to every virtue. In the same way, self-love, which destroys love and compassion toward one's neighbor, is the principle and foundation of every evil. All scandals, hatred, cruelty, and every sort of trouble issue from this perverse root of self-love. Such distorted self-love has poisoned the entire world, and has weakened the mystical body of the holy church and the universal body of the believers in the Christian religion. Therefore, all virtues grow out of the degree to which we love our neighbors. Indeed, love and compassion give life to all virtues. No virtue can be attained without compassion, which is the pure love of me.

"When the soul knows itself, it finds humility and hates its own sensual passion. It learns the perverse law that is part of its body and that always battles against its spirit. It begins to hate its own sensuality, fervently crushing it under the heel of reason. Then it discovers in itself the bounty of my goodness, because of the many benefits that I have given it. It then ponders these things in itself.

"In its humility, the soul attributes to me the knowledge of itself it has obtained. It knows that, by my grace, I have delivered it from darkness and lifted it up into the light of true knowledge.

"When the soul knows my goodness, it loves it both with and without a mediator. It loves it even without placing itself as mediator, or any other to its own advantage. But virtue is a mediator that it has conceived through its love of me. It sees that it can only become grateful and acceptable to me by hating sin and loving virtue. When the soul conceives virtue through loving compassion, it bears the fruit of virtue to its neighbor. It cannot act out the truth it has conceived in itself in any other way. It can only love me in truth, and in the same truth it serves its neighbor.

"And it cannot be otherwise, because love of me and of one's neighbor are one and the same thing; and, so far as the soul loves me, it loves its neighbor, because love towards one's neighbor issues from me. This is the means which I have given you, so that you may exercise and prove your virtue; because, inasmuch as you can do me no profit, you should do good to your neighbor. This proves that you possess me by grace in your soul, producing much fruit for your neighbor and making prayers to me, as you seek with sweet and loving desire my honor and the salvation of souls.

"The soul, enamored of my truth, never ceases to serve the whole world in general, and more or less in a particular case according to the disposition of the recipient and the ardent desire of the donor. For the endurance of suffering alone, without desire, is not sufficient to punish a fault.

"When the soul has discovered the advantage of this unitive love in me, by means of which it truly loves itself, extending its desire to the salvation of the whole world and thus coming to the aid of the world's neediness, it strives to fix its eye on the needs of its neighbor in particular.

"Therefore, it helps those who are at hand, according to the various graces which I have entrusted to it to administer. One it helps with doctrine, that is, with words, giving sincere counsel without any respect of persons. Another it helps with the example of a good life. Thus, indeed, all give to their neighbor the edification of a holy and honorable life.

"These are the virtues, along with many others too many to enumerate, which are brought forth in the love of one's neighbor. But, although I have given them in such a different way, that is to say not all to one, but one virtue to one, and another to another, it so happens that it is impossible to have one without having them all, because all the virtues are bound together.

"Learn, therefore that in many cases I give one virtue to be the chief of the others. That is to say, to one I will give principally love, to another principally justice, to another principally humility, or a lively faith, or prudence, or temperance, or patience, or fortitude. I could easily have created men possessed of all that they should need both for body and soul, but I desire that one should have need of the other, and that they should be my ministers to administer the graces and the gifts that they have received from me.

"Whether man desires to or not, he cannot help making an act of love. It is true, however, that that act, unless made through love of me, profits him nothing so far as grace is concerned. See then, that I have made men my ministers, and have placed them in differing stations and various ranks, in order that they may make use of the virtue of love.

"Therefore, I show you that in my house are many mansions, and that I wish for no other thing than love. For in the love of me is fulfilled and completed the love of one's neighbor, and the law is observed. For only those who are bound to me with this love, can be of use in their state of life."

How virtues are proved and strengthened by their opposites.

"Up to the present, I have taught you how one may serve one's neighbor, and manifest, by that service, the love which one has toward me. Now I wish to tell you further, that a man proves his patience by means of his neighbor when he receives injuries from him. Similarly, he proves his humility through a proud man, his faith through a faithless one, his true hope through one who despairs, his justice through the unjust, his kindness through the cruel, and his gentleness and graciousness through the irascible. Good men produce and prove all their virtues through their neighbor, just as perverse men do through all their vices.

"Thus, if you consider well, humility is proved against pride in that the humble man extinguishes pride, because a proud man can do no harm to a humble one. Neither can the lack of faith of a wicked man, who neither loves me nor hopes in me, when brought forth against one who is faithful to me, do him any harm; his faithlessness does not diminish the faith or the hope of one who has conceived his faith and hope through love of me. Rather, it strengthens and proves it in the love my servant feels for his neighbor. He sees that the faithless one is unfaithful because he is without hope in me, and because he does not love me. Such a one places his faith and hope rather in his own sensuality, which is all that he loves. My faithful and loving servant does not leave him, but instead, he extends to him my love and hope, which the other then has the choice of accepting or rejecting.

"And so it can be seen that virtues are developed, proved, and increased by their opposites in one's neighbors."

A TREATISE OF DISCRETION

*How the affection should not rely chiefly
on penance, but rather on virtues; and
how discretion receives life from humility,
and renders to each man his due.*

"I seek holy and sweet works from my servants.
These works are the proved, intrinsic virtues of
the soul. I desire more than exterior acts, done by
means of the body, or varied penances, which are the
instruments of virtue. Works of penance performed
alone, without the virtue of love, please me little.
Often a soul's perfection will be impeded if it performs acts of penance for the sake of penance and
not for love of me. It should rather rely on love of
me and of virtue, and on a holy hatred of itself,
accompanied by true humility and perfect patience,
as well as by hunger and desire for my honor and for
the salvation of souls. For these virtues demonstrate
that the will is dead, and continually slays its own
sensuality through the love of virtue.

"With this discretion, then, should the soul perform its penance, that is, it should place its principal affection in virtue rather than in penance. Penance should be but the means to increase virtue according to the needs of the individual, and according to what the soul sees it can do in the measure of its own possibility. Otherwise, if the soul places its foundation on penance, it will contaminate its own perfection, because its penance will not be done in the light of knowledge of itself and of my goodness, with discretion. It will not seize hold of my truth; neither will it love what I love, nor hate what I hate.

"This virtue of discretion is none other than a true knowledge that the soul should have of itself and of me. And in this knowledge is virtue rooted. Discretion is the only child of self-knowledge, and when it is wedded to charity it produces many virtues, as a tree makes many branches.

"That which gives life to this tree of discretion, to its branches of virtue, and to its root of self-knowledge is the ground of humility in which it is planted. For humility is the foster-mother of charity, and only through humility can this tree be sustained. Otherwise, this tree could not produce the virtue of discretion.

"The root of discretion is a real knowledge of self and of my goodness. By this knowledge the soul immediately, and discreetly, renders to each one his due, but chiefly to me in rendering praise and glory to my Name, and in referring to me all the graces and the gifts which it sees and knows it has received from me.

"It seems to itself to be ungrateful for so many benefits, and negligent in that it has not made the most of its time and of the graces it has received, and so it seems it is worthy of suffering. For these reasons it becomes odious and displeasing to itself through its guilt. And thus the virtue of discretion is founded on knowledge of self, that is, on true humility. For, if this humility were not in the soul, the soul would be indiscreet, because indiscretion is founded on pride, as discretion is on humility.

"An indiscreet soul robs me of the honor due to me, and attributes that honor to itself, through vainglory. And that which is really its own it imputes to me. It grieves and murmurs concerning my mysteries, with which I work in it and in the souls of my other creatures. Therefore everything in me and in the soul's neighbor is cause for scandal to it, contrary to the experience of those who possess the virtue of discretion.

"Discreet souls, on the other hand, when they have rendered what is due to me and to themselves, proceed to render to their neighbor their principal debt of love, and of humble and continuous prayer, which all should pay to each other. Further, they render to their neighbor the debt of doctrine and the example of a holy and honorable life, counseling and helping others according to their needs for salvation. Whatever rank a man may be in, whether that of a noble, a prelate, or a servant, if he has this virtue of discretion, everything that he does to his neighbor he does discreetly and lovingly, because these virtues are bound and mingled together. Both are planted in the ground of humility, which proceeds from self-knowledge."

A parable showing how love, humility, and discretion are united; and how the soul should conform itself to this parable.

"Do you know how the three virtues of love, humility, and discretion stand together? It is as if a circle were drawn on the surface of the earth, and a tree, with an off-shoot joined to its side, grew in the center of the circle. The tree is nourished in the earth contained in the diameter of the circle, for if the tree were out of the earth it would die and give no fruit.

"Now, consider, in the same way, that the soul is a tree existing by love, and that it can live by nothing else than love. And consider that if this soul does not have in very truth the divine love of perfect charity, it cannot produce fruit of life, but only of death.

"It is necessary then, that the root of this tree, that is the affection of the soul, should grow in, and issue from, the circle of true self-knowledge which is contained in me, who have neither beginning nor end, like the circumference of the circle. Turn as you will within a circle, inasmuch as the circumference has neither end nor beginning, you always remain within it.

"This knowledge of yourself and of me is found in the earth of true humility, which is as wide as the diameter of the circle, that is, as wide as the knowledge of self and of me. Otherwise, the circle would not be without an end and a beginning. It would have its beginning in knowledge of self, and its end in confusion, if this knowledge were not contained in me.

"Thus, the tree of love feeds on humility, bringing forth from its side the off-shoot of true discretion, from the heart of the tree. And true discretion is the affection of love in the soul, and the patience, proving that I am in the soul and the soul in me.

"This tree then, so sweetly planted, produces fragrant blossoms of virtue, with many scents of great variety, inasmuch as the soul renders the fruit of grace and of usefulness to its neighbor, according to the zeal of those who come to receive fruit from my servants. And to me it renders the sweet odor of glory and praise to my name, and so fulfills the object of its creation.

"In this way, therefore, the soul reaches the end and goal of its being, that is myself, its God, who am eternal Life. And these fruits cannot be taken from it without its will, inasmuch as they are all flavored with discretion, because they are all united."

How penance and other corporal exercises
are to be taken as instruments for arriving at
virtue, and not as the principal affection of
the soul; and how the light of discretion shines in
various other modes and operations.

"These are the fruits and the works that I seek
from the soul, namely, the proving of virtue in
the time of need. And yet some time ago, when you
wanted to do great penance for my sake, and asked,
'What can I do to endure suffering for you, Lord?' I
replied to you, 'I take delight in few words and
many works.'

"I wished to show you that one who merely calls
on me with the sound of words, saying: 'Lord, Lord,
I want to do something for you,' and one, who
desires for my sake to mortify his *body* with many
penances, but not his own *will*, do not give me much
pleasure. Instead, I desire the manifold works of
endurance with patience, together with the other
virtues intrinsic to the soul, all of which must be
active in order to obtain fruits worthy of grace.

"All other works, founded on any other principle
than this, I judge to be mere words. They are finite
works, and I, who am infinite, seek infinite works,
that is, an infinite perfection of love.

"I wish therefore that the works of penance and of
other corporal exercises, should be observed merely
as means to an end, and not as the fundamental

affection of the soul. For, if the principal affection of the soul were placed in penance, I should receive a finite thing like a word. Once a word has issued from the mouth, it is no more—unless it has issued with the affection of the soul, which conceives and brings forth virtue in truth. In other words, it is no more unless the finite operation, which I have called a word, should be joined with affection or love, in which case it would be pleasing to me.

"And this is because such a work would not be alone, but accompanied by true discretion, using corporal works as means, and not as the principal foundation. For it would not be becoming that the principal foundation should be placed in penance only, or in any exterior corporal act, for such works are finite, since they are done in finite time. It is often profitable for the creature to omit them, and even for it to be made to do so.

"Therefore, when the soul omits these works through necessity, being unable through various circumstances to complete an action that it has begun, or, as may frequently happen, through obedience at the order of its director, it is well. Indeed, if it continued then to do them, it not only would receive no merit, but would offend me. So you see that they are merely finite. Therefore, the soul ought to adopt them as a means, and not as an end. For, if it takes them as an end it will be obliged, some time or other, to leave them, and will then remain empty.

"This, my trumpeter, the glorious Paul, taught you when he said in his epistle that you should mortify the body and destroy self-will, knowing how to keep a rein on the body and to macerate the flesh whenever it wishes to combat the spirit. But the will should be dead and annihilated in everything, and subject to my will.

"And this slaying of the will, the virtue of discretion renders to the soul as its due. Discretion brings to the soul hatred and disgust of its own offenses and sensuality, which hatred it has acquired by self-knowledge. This is the knife that slays and cuts off all self-love founded in self-will. These then are the ones who give me not only words but manifold works, and in these I take delight.

"And then I said that I desired few words, and many actions. By the use of the word 'many,' I assign no particular number to you. That is because the affection of the soul, founded in love, which gives life to all virtues and good works, should increase infinitely. And yet by this I do not exclude words. I merely said that I wished few of them, showing you that every actual operation, as such, is finite, and therefore I called them of little account. But they please me when they are performed as the instruments of virtue, and not as a principal end in themselves.

"However, no one should judge that he has achieved greater perfection, because he performs great penances and gives himself in excess to the slaying of his body, than one who does less. For neither virtue nor merit consists in excess. Otherwise he would be in an evil state, who, for some legitimate reason, was unable to do actual penance. Merit consists in the virtue of love alone, flavored with the light of true discretion, without which the soul is worth nothing. And this love should be directed to me endlessly, boundlessly, since I am the supreme and eternal Truth.

"The soul can therefore place neither laws nor limits to its love for me. But its love for its neighbor, on the contrary, is limited by certain conditions. The light of discretion (which proceeds from love) gives to the neighbor a conditional love. Such a love, being ordered aright, does not cause the injury of sin to self in order to be useful to others. For, if one single sin were committed to save the whole world from hell, or to obtain one great virtue, the motive would not be a rightly ordered or discreet love, but rather indiscreet. For it is not lawful to perform even one act of great virtue and profit to others, by means of the guilt of sin.

"Holy discretion ordains that the soul should direct all its powers to my service with a manly zeal. It should love its neighbor with such devotion that it would lay down a thousand times, if it were possible, the life of its body for the salvation of souls. It should endure pains and torments so that its neighbor may have the life of grace, and give its temporal substance for the profit and relief of his body.

"This is the supreme office of discretion, which proceeds from charity. So you see how discreetly every soul who wishes for grace should pay its debts. That is, it should love me with an infinite love and without measure. But it should love its neighbor with measure, with a restricted love, not doing itself the injury of sin in order to be useful to others.

"This is St. Paul's counsel to you, when he says that charity ought to be concerned first with self, otherwise it will never be of perfect usefulness to others. And this is because, when perfection is not in the soul, everything the soul does for itself and for others is imperfect.

"It would not, therefore, be just that creatures, who are finite and created by me, should be saved through an offense done to me, the infinite Good. The more serious the fault is in such a case, the less fruit will the action produce. Therefore, in no way should you ever incur the guilt of sin.

"And this true love knows well, because it carries with itself the light of holy discretion, the light that dissipates all darkness. Discretion takes away ignorance and is the condiment of every instrument of virtue. Holy discretion is a prudence that cannot be cheated, a fortitude that cannot be beaten, a perseverance from end to end. It stretches from heaven to earth, that is, from knowledge of me to knowledge of self, and from love of me to love of others.

"The soul escapes dangers by its true humility. By its prudence it flies from all the nets of the world and its creatures. With unarmed hands, that is through much endurance, it discomfits the devil and the flesh with this sweet and glorious light. By this light of discretion, it knows its own fragility, and it renders to its weakness its due of hatred.

"Therefore the soul has trampled on the world and has placed it under the feet of her affection, despising it and holding it vile, and thus becoming lord of it. And the fools of the world cannot take the virtues from such a soul. Indeed, all their persecutions increase its virtues and prove them. These virtues are first conceived by the virtue of love, and then are proved through one's neighbor, bringing forth their fruit on him.

"Thus if virtue were not visible and did not shine in the time of trial, it would show that it was not truly conceived. Perfect virtue cannot exist and give fruit except by means of one's neighbor, even as a woman who has conceived a child, if she does not bring it forth so that it may appear before the eyes of all, deprives her husband of his fame of paternity. It is the same with me, the Spouse of the soul; if the soul does not produce its child of virtue in its love for its neighbor, showing its child to those in need, in truth, it has not conceived virtue at all. And this is also true of the vices, all of which are committed by means of the neighbor."

*How this servant of God grew by means
of the divine response, and how her sorrows
grew less; and how she prayed to God for the
holy church and for her own people.*

Then that servant of God thirsted and burned with
the very great desire that she had conceived on
learning the inexpressible love of God, as shown in
his great goodness. Seeing the breadth of his charity,
that, with such sweetness, he had deigned to reply to
her request and to satisfy it, gave hope to her sorrow
on account of offenses against God and the damage of
the holy church. This sight diminished, and yet, at the
same time, increased her sorrow.

For the supreme and eternal Father, in manifesting
the way of perfection, showed her anew her own guilt
and the loss of souls. Because of the knowledge that
this servant had obtained of herself, she knew more of
God. Knowing the goodness of God in herself, the
sweet mirror of God, she knew her own dignity and
indignity. Her dignity was that of her creation in the
image of God, and this dignity was given her by grace,
and not as her due.

In that same mirror of the goodness of God, this
servant knew her own indignity, which was the consequence of her own fault. Just as a one more readily
sees spots on one's face by looking in a mirror, so the
soul that, with true knowledge of self, rises with
desire and gazes with the eye of the intellect at itself

in the sweet mirror of God, knows better the stains
of its own face by the purity it sees in him.

Therefore, because light and knowledge
increased in that servant, a sweet sorrow grew in
her. At the same time, her sorrow was diminished
by the hope that the supreme Truth gave her. As
fire grows when it is fed with wood, so the fire
grew in that soul, to such an extent that it was no
longer possible for her body to endure it without
the departure of her soul. Had she not been sur-
rounded by the strength of him who is the supreme
Strength, it would not have been possible for her to
live any longer.

This servant then, being purified by the fire of
divine love, which she found in the knowledge of
herself and of God, and by her hunger for the salvation of the whole world and for the reformation of
the holy church, grew in her hope of obtaining her
desires. Therefore she rose with confidence before
the supreme Father and showed him the leprosy of
the holy church and the misery of the world, saying,
as if with the words of Moses, "Lord, turn the eyes
of your mercy upon your people and upon the mystical body of the holy church, for you will be the
more glorified if you forgive so many creatures and
give them the light of knowledge. For all will render
you praise when they see themselves escape through
your infinite goodness from the clouds of mortal sin,
and from eternal damnation. Then you will be
praised not only by my wretched self, who has so

much offended you, and who is the cause and the instrument of all this evil.

"Therefore I pray your divine and eternal love to take your revenge on me, and to show mercy to your people. Never will I depart from before your presence until I see that you grant them mercy.

"For what is it to me if I have life, and your people death, and the clouds of darkness cover your bride, the church, when it is my own sins, and not those of your other creatures, that are the principal cause of this? I desire, then, and beg of you, by your grace, that you have mercy on your people. I adjure you to do this by your uncreated love, which moved you to create man in your image and likeness, saying, 'Let us make man in our own image.' And you did this, eternal Trinity, so that mankind might participate in everything belonging to you, the most high and eternal Trinity.

"Therefore you gave us memory, in order to receive your benefits, by which we participate in the power of the eternal Father. You gave us intellect, that we might know, seeing your goodness, and might participate in the wisdom of your only-begotten Son. And you gave us will, that we might love that which our intellect has seen and known of your truth, and thus participate in the clemency of your Holy Spirit.

"What reason did you have for creating man in such dignity? It was the inestimable love with which you saw your creature in yourself, and became enamored of him. For you created him through love, and destined him to be such that he might taste and enjoy your eternal Good. I see, therefore, that through his sin he lost this dignity in which you originally placed him, and by his rebellion against you fell into a state of war with your kindness. That is to say, we all became your enemies.

"Therefore, moved by that same fire of love with which you created him, you willingly gave man a means of reconciliation, so that after the great rebellion into which he had fallen, there should come a great peace. And so you gave him the only-begotten Word, your Son, to be the mediator between us and you. He was our Justice, for he took on himself all our offenses and injustices, and performed your obedience, eternal Father, which you imposed on him when you clothed him with our humanity, our human nature, and our likeness.

"Oh, abyss of love! What heart can help breaking when it sees such dignity as yours descend to such lowliness as our humanity? We are your image, and you have become ours, by this union which you have accomplished with man, veiling the eternal Deity with the cloud of woe and the corrupted clay of Adam. For what reason?—Love. Therefore, you, God, have become man, and man has become God. By this inexpressible love of yours, therefore, I constrain you, and implore you, that you show mercy to your creatures."

How sin is more gravely punished after the Passion
of Christ than before; and how God promises to show
mercy to the world and to the holy church, by means
of the prayers and sufferings of his servants.

"I wish you to know, my daughter, that, although I
have re-created and restored the human race to the
life of grace through the blood of my only-begotten
Son, men are not grateful. They go from bad to
worse and from guilt to guilt, even persecuting me
with many injuries. They take so little account of the
graces that I have given them and continue to give
them, that, not only do they not attribute to grace
what they have received, but they believe themselves
on occasion to receive injuries from me, as if I
desired anything else than their sanctification.

"I say to you that they will be more hard-hearted,
and worthy of more punishment, and will, indeed,
be punished more severely, now that they have
received redemption in the blood of my Son, than
they would have been before that redemption took
place—that is, before the stain of Adam's sin was
taken away. It is right that one who receives more
should give more back, and should be under great
obligation to him from whom he receives more.

"Man, then, was closely bound to me through
his being, which I gave him, creating him in my own
image and likeness. For that reason he was bound to
render me glory; but he deprived me of it, and

wished to give it to himself. Thus he came to transgress my obedience imposed on him, and became my enemy. And I destroyed his pride with my humility, humiliating the divine nature and taking your humanity. And, freeing you from the service of the devil, I made you free.

"Not only did I give you liberty, but if you will examine, you will see that man has become God and God has become man, through the union of the divine with the human nature. This is the debt that men have incurred—the treasure of the Blood, by which they have been procreated to grace.

"See, therefore, how much more men owe after the redemption than before. They are now obliged to render me glory and praise by following in the steps of my incarnate Word, my only-begotten Son, for then they repay me the debt of love both of myself and of their neighbor, with true and genuine virtue. And if they do not do it, the greater will be their debt, and the greater will be the offense they fall into. Therefore, by divine justice, the greater will be their suffering in eternal damnation.

"A false Christian is punished more than a pagan, and the deathless fire of divine justice consumes him more, that is, afflicts him more. In his affliction, he feels himself being consumed by the worm of conscience, though, in truth, he is not consumed, because the damned do not lose their being through any torment that they receive. Therefore I say to you that they ask for death and cannot have it, for they cannot lose their being. The existence of grace they lose, through their fault, but not their natural existence.

"Therefore, guilt is more gravely punished after the redemption of the Blood than before, because man received more. But sinners neither seem to perceive this, nor to pay any attention to their own sins. And so they become my enemies, though I have reconciled them by means of the blood of my Son.

"But there is a remedy with which I appease my wrath—that is, by means of my servants, if they are jealous to constrain me by their desire. You see, therefore, that you have bound me with this bond which I have given you, because I wished to show mercy to the world.

"Therefore I give my servants hunger and desire for my honor, and the salvation of souls, so that, constrained by their tears, I may mitigate the fury of my divine justice. Therefore, take your tears and your sweat, drawn from the fountain of my divine love, and with them, wash the face of my bride, the church.

"I promise you that, by this means, my bride's beauty will be restored to her, not by the knife nor by cruelty, but peacefully, by humble and continued prayer, by the sweat and the tears shed by the fiery desire of my servants. Thus will I fulfill your desire, if you, on your part, endure much, and cast the light of your patience into the darkness of perverse man. Do not fear the world's persecutions, since I will protect you. My Providence shall never fail you in the slightest need."

How, the road to heaven was broken through the disobedience of Adam, but God made of his Son a bridge by which man could pass.

"I have told you that I have made a bridge of my Word, my only-begotten Son, and this is the truth. I wish for you, my children, to know that the road was broken by the sin and disobedience of Adam, in such a way that no one could arrive at eternal Life. Therefore men did not render me glory in the way in which they ought to have, as they did not participate in that good for which I had created them, and my truth was not fulfilled.

"This truth is that I have created man in my own image and likeness, so that he might have eternal life, and might partake of me and taste my supreme and eternal sweetness and goodness. But after sin had closed heaven and bolted the doors of mercy, the soul of man produced thorns and prickly brambles, and my creature found in himself rebellion against himself.

"The flesh immediately began to war against the Spirit, and losing the state of innocence, it became a foul animal. Then all created things rebelled against man, whereas they would have been obedient to him if he had remained in the state in which I had placed him. But not remaining in that state, he transgressed my obedience, and became worthy of eternal death in soul and body.

"As soon as he had sinned, there arose a tempestuous flood which continues to buffet him with its waves, bringing him weariness and trouble from himself, the devil, and the world. Everyone was drowned in the flood, because no one, with his own righteousness alone, could arrive at eternal life. And so, wishing to remedy your great evils, I have given you the bridge of my Son, so that you may pass across the flood—the tempestuous sea of this dark life—and not be drowned. See, therefore, under what obligation the creature is to me, and how ignorant he is not to take the remedy that I have offered, but to be willing to drown."

How God induces the soul to look at the greatness of this bridge, which reaches from earth to heaven.

"Open, my daughter, the eye of your intellect, and you will see the accepted and the ignorant, the imperfect, and also the perfect who follow me in truth, so that you may grieve over the damnation of the ignorant and rejoice over the perfection of my beloved servants.

"You will see further how those who walk in the light carry themselves, and how those who walk in the darkness carry themselves. I also want you to look at the bridge of my only-begotten Son and see its greatness. That is, that by it the earth of your humanity is joined to the greatness of the Deity, for it reaches from heaven to earth. I say then that this bridge constitutes the union that I have made with man.

"This bridge was necessary in order to re-form the road that was broken, so that man could pass through the bitterness of the world and arrive at life. But the bridge could not be made of sufficient earth to span the flood and give you eternal life, because the earth of human nature was not sufficient to remove the stain of Adam's sin, which corrupted the whole human race and gave out a stench.

"Therefore, it was necessary to join human nature with the loftiness of my nature, the eternal Deity, making it sufficient to satisfy for the whole human race. Only in this way could human nature sustain the punishment, and the divine nature, united with the human, could make acceptable the sacrifice of my only Son, offered to me to take death from you and to give you life.

"So the loftiness of the divinity, humbled to the earth and joined with your humanity, made the bridge and re-formed the road. Why was this done? So that man might come to his true happiness with the angels. Observe, however, that it is not enough that my Son made you this bridge so that you could have life, unless you are willing to walk on it."

How this servant prays God to show her those who cross by the bridge, and those who do not.

Then this servant exclaimed with ardent love— "Inestimable charity, sweet above all sweetness! Who would not be inflamed by such great love? What heart can help breaking at such tenderness? It seems, abyss of charity, as if you were mad with love of your creature, as if you could not live without him—and yet you are our God who has no need of us. Your greatness does not increase through our good, for you are unchangeable, and our evil causes you no harm, for you are the supreme and eternal Goodness. What moves you to show us such mercy through pure love, and not on account of any debt that you owed us or need that you had of us? We are rather your guilty and malignant debtors.

"Therefore, if I understand rightly, supreme and eternal Truth, I am the thief and you have been punished for me. For I see your Word, your Son, fastened and nailed to the cross. Of him you have made a Bridge for me, your miserable servant. For this reason, my heart is bursting, and yet cannot burst, through the hunger and the desire that it has conceived towards you. I remember, Lord, that you were willing to show me those who go by the bridge and those who do not. Should it please your Goodness to manifest this to me, willingly would I see and hear it."

How this bridge has three steps, which signify the three states of the soul; and how, being lifted on high, yet it is not separated from the earth; and how these words are to be understood: "If I am lifted up from the earth, I will draw all things unto me."

Then the eternal God, to excite that servant still more for the salvation of souls, replied to her: "First, I will explain to you the nature of this bridge. I have told you, my daughter, that the bridge reaches from heaven to earth, through the union which I have made with man, whom I formed out of the clay of the earth. Now learn that this bridge, my only-begotten Son, has three steps, of which two were made with the wood of the most holy cross. And the third still retains the great bitterness he tasted when he was given gall and vinegar to drink.

"In these three steps you will recognize three states of the soul, which I will explain to you. The feet of the soul, signifying its affection, are related to the first step of the bridge, my only-begotten Son. This step is his feet, for the feet carry the body, as the affection carries the soul. These pierced feet are the step by which you can arrive at his side, which is the second step.

"The second step manifests to you the secret of his heart, because the soul, rising on the step of its affection, begins to taste the love of his heart. Gazing into that open heart of my Son with the eye of the intellect, the soul finds it consumed with inexpressible love. I say consumed, because he does not love you for his own profit. Indeed you can be of no profit to him, for he is one and the same thing with me. Then the soul is filled with love, at seeing itself so much loved.

"Having passed the side, which is the second step, the soul reaches out to the third—that is, to the mouth, where it finds peace from the terrible war it has been waging with its sin. On the first step, then, lifting its feet from the affections of the earth, the soul strips itself of vice; on the second it fills itself with love and virtue; and on the third it tastes peace.

"So the bridge has three steps, in order that, climbing past the first and the second, you may reach the last, which is lifted on high. For that reason the water, running beneath, may not touch it, for in my Son there was no poison of sin. This bridge is lifted on high, and yet, at the same time, it remains joined to the earth. Do you know when it was lifted on high? When my Son was lifted up on the wood of the most holy cross, the divine nature remaining joined to the lowliness of the earth of your humanity.

"This is why I said to you that, being lifted on high, he was not lifted out of the earth: For the divine nature is united and kneaded into one thing with it. And there was no one who could go on the bridge until it had been lifted on high. Therefore he said, 'If I am lifted on high I will draw all things to me.'

"My eternal goodness saw that in no other way could you be drawn to me, so I sent him in order that he should be lifted on high on the wood of the cross. Thus the cross was made into an anvil on which my Son, born of human generation, should be re-made, in order to free you from death and to restore you to the life of grace. He drew everything to himself by this means, namely, by showing the inexpressible love with which I love you, since the heart of man is always attracted by love. Greater love I could not show you, than to lay down my life for you. It was necessary, then, for my Son to be treated in this way by love, in order that ignorant man should be unable to resist being drawn to me.

"In very truth, then, my Son said that, being lifted on high, he would draw all things to himself. And this is to be understood in two ways. First, when the heart of man is drawn by the affection of love, it is drawn together with all the powers of his soul—that is, with the memory, the intellect, and the will. Now, when these three powers are harmoniously joined together in my name, all the other operations that the man performs, whether in deed or thought, are pleasing and joined together by the effect of love. This is the result of love being lifted on high, fol-lowing the sorrowful, crucified One. So my Truth said well, 'If I am lifted on high I will draw all things to me.' For, if one's heart and the powers of the soul are drawn to him, all one's actions are also drawn to him.

"Second, everything has been created for the service of mankind, to serve the necessities of rational creatures. The rational creature has not been made for things, but for me, in order to serve me with all his heart and with all his affection. Since man is drawn, everything else is drawn with him, because everything else has been made for him. It was therefore necessary for the bridge to be lifted on high, and to have steps, in order that it might be climbed more easily."

How this bridge is built of stones that signify virtues; and how on the bridge is an inn where food is given to the travelers; and how those who go over the bridge go to life, while those who go under it go to perdition and death.

"This bridge is built of stones, so that, if the rain comes, it may not impede the traveler. Do you know what these stones are? They are the stones of true and sincere virtues. These stones were not built into the walls before the Passion of my Son, and therefore even those who attempted to walk by the road of virtue were prevented from arriving at their journey's end. Heaven was not yet unlocked with the key of the Blood, and justice did not let them pass.

"But after the stones were made and built up on the body of my sweet Son, my Word, he who was himself the bridge moistened the mortar for its building with his blood. That is, his blood was united with the mortar of divinity, and with the strength and the fire of love. By my power, these stones of the virtues were built into a wall. He was the foundation, for there is no virtue that has not been proved in him, and from him all virtues have their life.

"Therefore no one can have the virtue given by a life of grace, except from him, that is, without following the footsteps of his doctrine. He has built a wall made of the virtues, planting them as living stones and cementing them with his blood. Now every believer may walk speedily and without any servile fear of divine justice, for he is sheltered by the mercy that descended from heaven in the incarnation of my Son. How was heaven opened? With the key of his blood. So you see that the bridge is walled and roofed with mercy.

"His also is the inn in the garden of the holy church. For the church keeps and ministers the bread of life and gives to drink of the blood, so that my creatures, journeying on their pilgrimage, may not become weary and faint by the way. For this reason my love has ordained that the blood and the body of my only-begotten Son, wholly God and wholly man, may be ministered to you.

"Having crossed the bridge, the pilgrim arrives at a door at the end of it; by this door all must enter. For that reason my Son says, 'I am the way, the truth, and the life; he who follows me does not walk in darkness, but in light.' And in another place my Truth says that no man can come to me if not by him. Therefore he says of himself that he is the road. This is the truth: He is the road in the form of a bridge.

"He also says that he is the truth. And so he is, because he is united with me who am the Truth. Those who follow him walk in the truth and in life, because those who follow this truth receive the life of grace, and cannot faint from hunger: The Truth has become their food. Nor can they fall in the darkness, because he is light without any falsehood. With that Truth, he confounded and destroyed the lie that the devil told to Eve, breaking up the road to heaven. The Truth brought the pieces together again and cemented them with his blood. Those who follow this road are the children of the Truth, because they follow the Truth. They pass through the door of Truth and find themselves united to me, who am the door and the road, and at the same time infinite peace.

"But those who do not walk on this road go under the bridge, in the river where there are no stones, only water. Since there are no supports in the water, no one can travel that way without drowning. Thus have come to pass the sins and the condition of the world. If the soul places affection, not on the stones, but with disordinate love on creatures, loving them and being kept by them far from me, the soul drowns. For creatures are like water that continually runs past. Man also passes continually like the river, although it seems to him that he stands still and the creatures that he loves pass by. Yet he is passing himself continually to the end of his journey—death!

"Man would gladly hold onto himself (that is his life, and the things that he loves). But he does not succeed, either through death, by which he has to leave these things, or through my disposition, by which these created things are taken from the sight of my creatures. Such men follow a lie, and walk on the road of falsehood. They are sons of the devil, who is the father of lies. Because they pass through the door of falsehood, they receive eternal damnation. So, then, I have shown you both truth and falsehood: my road, which is truth, and the devil's, which is falsehood."

How traveling on both of these roads, that is the bridge and the river, is fatiguing; and of the delight which the soul feels in traveling by the bridge.

"These are the two roads, and both are hard to travel. Wonder, then, at the ignorance and blindness of man. Having a road made for him that causes such delight to those who use it that every bitterness becomes sweet and every burden light, he prefers to walk in the water. Those who cross by the bridge, being still in the darkness of the body, find light. Being mortal, they find immortal life. Through love, they taste the light of eternal truth, which promises refreshment to those who weary themselves for me. For I am grateful and just, and render to every man according to what he deserves.

"Therefore every good deed is rewarded, and every fault is punished. The tongue would not be sufficient to relate the delight felt by those who follow this road of truth, for, even in this life, they taste and participate in the good that has been prepared for them in eternal life. Therefore, they are fools indeed, who despise so great a good, and choose rather to receive in this life the pledge of hell. Walking by the lower road with great toil, they have neither refreshment nor advantage. Through their sins, they are deprived of me, the supreme and eternal Good. Truly, then, you have reason for grief. And it is my will that you and my other servants remain in continual bitterness of soul at the offense done to me, and in compassion for the ignorant, and those who are lost by offending me in their ignorance.

"Now you have seen and heard about this bridge and what it is like. And I have told you this in order to explain my saying that my only-begotten Son was a bridge. So you see that he is the Truth, made in the way that I have shown you, that is, by the union of height and lowliness."

How this bridge, having reached to heaven
on the day of the Ascension, did not for
that reason leave the earth.

"When my only-begotten Son returned to me forty days after the Resurrection, he, the bridge, arose from the earth, and from living among men, and ascended into heaven. By virtue of the divine nature he sat at the right hand of me, the eternal Father. This is what the angels said on the day of the Ascension to the disciples, as they stood like dead men: 'Do not stand here any longer, for he is seated at the right hand of the Father!'

"When he had ascended on high and returned to me, the Father, I sent the teacher, that is, the Holy Spirit. The Spirit came to you with my power and with the wisdom of my Son, and with his own clemency, which is the essence of the Holy Spirit. He is one with me, the Father, and with my Son. And he built up the road of the doctrine which my Truth had left in the world. In this way, though the bodily presence of my Son left you, his doctrine remained, as did the virtue of the stones founded upon this doctrine—which is the way made for you by this bridge.

"First, he practiced this doctrine himself and made the road by his actions. He gave you his doctrine by example rather than by words. Only afterwards did he teach his doctrine to the disciples. The Holy Spirit's clemency made them certain of the doctrine and strengthened their minds to confess the truth and to announce this road, that is, the doctrine of Christ crucified. In this way he reproved the world of its injustice and false judgment. I have said this much to you so there might be no cloud of darkness in the mind of your hearers. That is, I want them to know that of Christ's body, I made a bridge by the union of the divine with the human nature.

"Taking its point of departure in you, this bridge rose into heaven. This was the one road that the example and life of the Truth taught you. What now remains of all this? Where is the road to be found? I tell you that this way of his doctrine, confirmed by the apostles, declared by the blood of the martyrs, illuminated by the light of doctors, confessed by the confessors, narrated in all its love by the evangelists—all of whom stand as witnesses to confess the Truth—is found in the mystical body of the holy church.

"These witnesses are like the light placed on a candlestick to show forth the way of the Truth which leads to life with a perfect light. And as they themselves say to you and have proved in their own cases, every person may, if he chooses, be illuminated to know the Truth—unless through his inordinate self-love he chooses to deprive his reason of light. It is indeed the truth that his doctrine is true. And this doctrine remains like a lifeboat to draw souls out of the tempestuous sea and to conduct them to the port of salvation.

"For this reason I first gave you the bridge of my Son, living and conversing in very deed amongst men. When he, the living Bridge, left you, there remained the bridge and the road of his doctrine, joined with my power and his wisdom, and with the clemency of the Holy Spirit. This power of mine gives the virtue of strength to those who follow this road. Wisdom gives them light, so that in this road, they may recognize the truth. And the Holy Spirit gives them love, which consumes and takes away all love of the senses out of the soul, leaving only the love of virtue.

"Therefore, both actually and through his doctrine, he is the way, the truth, and the life. In other words, he is the bridge that leads you to heaven. This is what he meant when he said, 'I came from the Father, and I return to the Father, and shall return to you.' That is to say, 'My Father sent me to you and made me your bridge, so that you might be saved from the river and attain life.' Then he says, 'I will return to you. I will not leave you orphans, but will send you the Paraclete.' It is as if my Truth were saying, 'I will go to the Father and return; that is, that when the Holy Spirit comes, the One called the Paraclete, he will show you more clearly, and will confirm you in the way of truth that I have given you.' He said that he would return, and he did return, because the Holy Spirit did not come alone, but with the power of the Father, the wisdom of the Son, and the clemency of his own essence.

"See then how he returns, not in actual flesh and blood, but building the road of his doctrine with his power. And that road cannot be destroyed or taken away from those who wish to follow it, because it is firm and stable, and it proceeds from me, who am immovable. You should follow this road manfully, then, without any cloud of doubt, but with the light of faith that was given you as a principle in holy baptism.

"Now I have fully shown to you the bridge as it actually is, and the doctrine that is one and the same thing with it. And I have shown it to the ignorant, so that they may see where this road of truth is, and where those who teach it stand. These are the apostles, martyrs, confessors, evangelists, and holy doctors, placed like lanterns in the holy church.

"My Son, returned to me, but none the less, he returned to you—not in his bodily presence, but by his power, when the Holy Spirit came upon the disciples. He will not return in his bodily presence until the last day of judgment, when he will come again with my majesty and divine power to judge the world. Then he will render good to the virtuous and reward them for their labors both in body and soul. And he will dispense the evil of eternal death to those who have lived wickedly in the world.

"And now I wish to tell you what I, the Truth, promised you. That is, I will show you the perfect, the imperfect, and the supremely perfect. And I will show you the wicked who, through their iniquities, drown in the river, attaining to punishment and torment. For this reason I say to you, my dearest children, walk over the bridge and not underneath it. For underneath is not the way of truth, but the way of falsehood used by the wicked. These are the sinners for whom I beg you to pray to me and for whom I ask your tears and sweat, so that they may receive mercy from me."

How this servant, wondering at the mercy of God, relates many gifts and graces given to the human race.

Then this servant, like an intoxicated person, could not contain herself. Standing before the face of God, she exclaimed, "How great is the eternal mercy with which you cover the sins of your creatures! I do not wonder that you say of those who abandon mortal sin and return to you, 'I do not remember that you have ever offended me.' Inexpressible mercy! No wonder you say to the converted, speaking of those who persecute you, 'I want you to pray for so-and-so, in order that I may show them mercy.'

"Mercy, you proceed from your eternal Father; divinity, with your power you govern the whole world: By you we were created, in you we were re-created in the blood of your Son. Your mercy preserves us; your mercy caused your Son to do battle for us,

hanging by his arms on the wood of the cross, life and
death battling together. Then life confounded the
death of our sin, and the death of our sin destroyed
the bodily life of the immaculate Lamb. Which one
was finally conquered? Death! By what means?
Mercy!

"Your mercy gives light and life. By it your
clemency is known in all your creatures, both the
just and the unjust. In the height of heaven your
mercy shines in your saints. If I turn to the earth, it
abounds with your mercy. In the darkness of hell
your mercy shines, for the damned do not receive the
pains they deserve; you temper justice with your
mercy. By mercy you have washed us in the Blood,
and by mercy you desire to converse with your
creatures.

"Loving Madman! Was it not enough for you to
take on human flesh, that you must also die? Was
not death enough, that you must also descend into
Limbo, taking out of it the holy fathers, in order to
fulfill your mercy and your truth in them? Because
your goodness promises a reward to those who serve
you in truth, you descended to Limbo, in order to
withdraw your servants from their pain and to give
them the fruit of their labors.

"Your mercy constrains you to give even more to
mortals, namely, to leave yourself to them in food.
In this way we weak ones have comfort, and the
ignorant, by commemorating you, do not lose the
memory of your benefits.

"For this reason, every day you give yourself to man, representing yourself in the sacrament of the altar, in the body of your holy church. What has done this? Your mercy. Oh, divine mercy! My heart suffocates in thinking of you, for everywhere I turn my thoughts, I find nothing but mercy. Eternal Father! Forgive my ignorance that makes me presume to chatter to you. The love of your mercy will be my excuse before the face of your loving-kindness."

Of the baseness of those who pass by the river under the bridge; and how the soul that passes underneath, is called by God the tree of death, the roots of which are held in four vices.

After this servant had refreshed her heart in the mercy of God by these words, she humbly waited for the fulfillment of the promise made to her. Then God continued his discourse:

"Dearest daughter, you have spoken to me of my mercy, because I gave it to you to taste and to see in the word I spoke to you: 'These are the ones for whom I plead with you to intercede with me.' But know that my mercy is beyond comprehension, far more than you can see, because your sight is imperfect, but my mercy is perfect and infinite. So there can be no relating between the two except what relating there may be between a finite and an infinite thing.

"But I have desired you to taste this mercy and also the dignity of mankind so that you might know better the cruelty of those wicked ones who travel below the bridge. Open the eye of your intellect, and wonder at those who drown themselves voluntarily. Wonder at the baseness to which they are fallen through their fault. For first they become weak and conceive mortal sin in their minds, and then they bring it forth and lose the life of grace. Just as a corpse can have no feeling or movement in itself, so those who are drowned in the stream of disordinate love of the world and of themselves, are dead to the feeling and movement of grace.

"Because they are dead to grace, their memory takes no notice of my mercy. The eye of their intellect neither sees nor knows my truth. And their will is dead to my will, because it loves nothing but dead things. Since these three powers are dead, namely the memory, the intellect, and the will, all the soul's operations both in deed and thought are dead as far as grace is concerned. For the soul cannot defend herself against its enemies, nor help itself through its own power, but only inasmuch as it is helped by me and my grace.

"Free will, which remains as long as the mortal body lives, is the only thing remaining in this corpse. So it is true that every time this corpse asks for my help, he can have it, but never can he help himself. He has become intolerable to himself. He wants to govern the world, but is governed by that which is not, that is by sin, for in itself sin is nothing. Such people have become the servants and slaves of sin. I have made them trees of love with the life of grace, which they received in holy baptism. But they have become trees of death, because they are dead.

"Do you know how these trees find such roots of death? In the loftiness of pride, nourished by their own sensitive self-love. Their branches are their own impatience and its offshoot, indiscretion. These, then, are the four principal vices that destroy the soul of those who are trees of death, because they have not drawn life from grace: pride, self-love, impatience, and indiscretion.

"Inside the tree the worm of conscience is nourished. But while man lives in mortal sin, the conscience is blinded by self-love, and therefore is felt but little. The fruits of this tree are mortal, for instead of drawing their nourishment from humility, they have drawn it from the roots of pride. Thus the miserable soul is full of ingratitude, from which proceeds every evil. If the soul were grateful for the benefits it has received, it would know me. Knowing me, it would know itself, and so would remain in my love. But the soul, as if blind, goes groping down the river, and it does not see that the water does not support it."

How the fruits of this tree of death are as diverse as are sins; and first, of the sin of sensuality.

"The fruits of this death-giving tree are as diverse as sins are diverse. Some of these fruits are the food of beasts that live impurely, using their body and mind like a swine that wallows in mud—for in the same way they wallow in the mire of sensuality. Ugly soul, where have you left your dignity? You were made sister to the angels, and now you have become a brute beast. Sinners come to such misery, despite the fact that they are sustained by me, who am supreme purity, and despite the fact that the devils themselves, whose friends and servants they have become, cannot endure the sight of such filthy actions.

"No sin, abominable as it may be, takes away the light of the intellect from mankind, so much as does this one of sensuality. The philosophers knew this, not by the light of grace, which they lacked, but because nature gave them the light to know that this sin obscured the intellect. For that reason they preserved themselves in continence, the better to study. For the same reason they flung away their riches, so that the thought of them would not occupy their heart. Not so does the ignorant and false Christian, who has lost grace by sin."

How the other fruits include avarice; and
the evils that proceed from it.

"The fruit of avarice belongs to some who are cov-
etous misers. They act like the mole, who
always feeds on earth till death; and when they
arrive at death they find no remedy. Such people,
with their pettiness, despise my generosity, selling
time to their neighbor. They are cruel usurers and
robbers of their neighbor. In their memory they have
no remembrance of my mercy, for if they had it, they
would not be cruel to themselves or to their neighbor. On the contrary, they would be compassionate
and merciful to themselves, and would practice the
virtues on their neighbor and assist him charitably.

"How many are the evils that come of this
cursed sin of avarice! How many homicides and
thefts! How much pillage with unlawful gain, how
much cruelty of heart and injustice! Avarice kills the
soul and makes it the slave of riches, so that it does
not care to observe my commandments.

"Misers love no one except for their own profit.
Their avarice proceeds from and feeds their pride.
The one follows the other, because misers always
carry with them the thought of their own reputation.
Thus avarice, which is immediately combined with
pride, full of its own opinions, goes on from bad to
worse. It is a fire that always gives rise to the smoke

of vainglory and vanity of heart, and of boasting in that which does not belong to it.

"Avarice is a root that has many entangling branches, and the principal one makes people care for their own reputation. From this branch proceeds their desire to be greater than their neighbor. It also brings forth a deceitful heart that is neither pure nor liberal, but is double-minded. Such a heart makes people show one thing with their tongue, while they have another in their heart. It makes them conceal the truth and tell lies for their own profit. And it produces envy, which is a worm that is always gnawing, never letting misers have any happiness out of their own or others' good.

"How will these wicked ones in so wretched a state give of their substance to the poor, when they rob others? How will they draw their foul souls out of the mire, when they themselves put them there? Sometimes they even become so brutish that they do not consider their children and relatives, and cause them to fall with them into great misery. Nevertheless, in my mercy I sustain them; I do not command the earth to swallow them up, so they may repent of their sins.

"Would they then give their life for the salvation of souls, when they will not give their substance? Would they give their affections, when they are gnawed with envy? Miserable vices that destroy the heaven of the soul! Heaven I call the soul, because so I made it, living in it at first by grace, and hiding myself within it, and making of it a mansion through affection of love. Now it has separated itself from me, like an adulteress, loving itself and creatures more than me. It has made a god of itself, persecuting me with many sins. And it does this because it does not consider the benefit of the Blood that was shed with so great a fire of love."

How some others hold positions of authority,
and bring forth fruits of injustice.

"There are others who hold their heads high by their position of authority, and who bear the banner of injustice. They use injustice against their neighbor, against themselves, and against me, God—against themselves by not paying the debt of virtue, and against me by not paying the debt of honor in glorifying and praising my name, which debt they are bound to pay.

"Like thieves, they steal what is mine and give it to the service of their own sensuality, so that they commit injustice towards me and towards themselves. They are like blind and ignorant ones who do not recognize me in themselves on account of self-love. They are like the Jews and the ministers of the Law, who with envy and self-love blinded themselves so that they did not recognize the Truth, my only-begotten Son. They did not render his due to the eternal Truth who was amongst them. Indeed, my Truth said, 'The kingdom of God is among you.' But they did not know it, because they had lost the light of reason. And so they did not pay their debt of honor and glory to me, and to him, who was one thing with me. Like blind ones, they committed injustice, persecuting him with much ignominy, even to the death of the cross.

"Thus such as these are unjust to their neighbor, to themselves, and to me. Unjustly they sell the flesh of their dependents, and of any person who falls into their hands."

*How through these and through other defects,
one falls into false judgment; and of the
indignity to which one comes.*

"By these and by other sins, men fall into false judgment. They are continually scandalized by my works, which are all just, and all performed in truth through love and mercy. With this false judgment, and with the poison of envy and pride, men slandered and unjustly judged the works of my Son. With lies his enemies said, 'This man works by virtue of Beelzebub.' Thus wicked men, standing in self-love, impurity, pride, and avarice, and operating out of envy and perverse rashness with impatience, are forever scandalized at me and at my servants.

Because their heart is rotten, and its rottenness having spoiled their taste, they judge my servants to be feignedly practicing the virtues. Good things seem evil to them, and bad things, that is to say disorderly living, seem good to them.

"How blind is the human generation, in that it does not consider its own dignity! From being great you have become small. From a ruler you have become a slave, and that in the vilest service that can be had. Because you are the servant and slave of sin, you have become like that which you serve.

"Sin is nothing. You, then, have become nothing; sin has deprived you of life and given you death. This life and power were given to you by the Word, my only-begotten Son, the glorious Bridge. He drew you from out of your slavery when you were slaves of the devil, becoming as a slave himself to take you out of slavery. He imposed on himself obedience in order to do away with the disobedience of Adam, and humbled himself to the shameful death of the cross in order to confound pride.

"By his death he destroyed every vice, so that no one could say that any vice remained that was not punished and beaten out with pains, for of his Body he made an anvil. All the remedies are ready to save men from eternal death. Yet they despise the Blood and trample it under the feet of their disordinate affection. It is for this injustice and false judgment that the world is rebuked, and will be rebuked on the last day of judgment.

"This is what my Truth meant when he said, 'I will send the Paraclete, who will rebuke the world of injustice and false judgment.' And I rebuked the world when I sent the Holy Spirit on the apostles."

Of the words that Christ said: "I will send the Holy Spirit, who will rebuke the world of injustice and of false judgment"; and how the first of these rebukes is continuous.

"There are three rebukes of injustice and false judgment. One was given when the Holy Spirit came upon the disciples. They, being fortified by my power and illuminated by the wisdom of my beloved Son, received all in the fullness of the Holy Spirit. The Holy Spirit, who is one with me and with my Son, rebuked the world, through the mouth of the apostles, with the doctrine of my Truth. They and all others who are descended from them, following the truth which they understand through the same means, rebuke the world.

"This is the continuous rebuke that I make to the world by means of the Holy Scriptures and by my servants. I put the Holy Spirit on their tongues to announce my truth, even as the devil puts himself on the tongues of his servants, that is, on the tongues of those who pass through the river in iniquity. This is the sweet rebuke that I have fixed forever out of my great love for the salvation of souls. And they cannot say, 'I had no one who rebuked me,' because the truth is revealed to them, and it shows them vice and virtue.

"I have made men see the fruit of virtue and the hurtfulness of vice, to give them love and holy fear so they may hate vice and love virtue. And this truth has not been shown them by an angel, so they cannot say, 'The angel is a blessed spirit who cannot offend, and does not feel the vexations of the flesh as we do, nor the heaviness of our body.' No, it was in your mortal flesh that I gave the incarnate Word of my Truth.

"Who were the others who followed this Word? Mortal creatures, susceptible to pain like you, having the same opposition of the flesh to the Spirit. Among them were the glorious Paul, my standard-bearer, and many other saints. By one thing or another they were tormented with torments that I permitted so that grace and virtue might increase in their souls. They were born in sin like you, and were nourished with similar food.

"I am God now as then. My power is not weakened, and cannot become weak. Therefore I can and will help those who want me to help them. Men show that they want my help when they come out of the river and walk by the bridge, following the doctrine of my Truth.

"Therefore no one has any excuse, because both rebukes and truth are constantly given to them. As a result, if they do not change their lives while they have time, they will be condemned by the second condemnation that will take place at the extremity of death. Then my justice will cry to them, 'Rise, you dead, and come to judgment!' In other words, 'You who are dead to grace and have reached the moment of your corporal death, rise and come before the supreme Judge with your injustice and false judgment. Come with the extinguished light of faith, which you received burning in holy baptism (and which you have blown out by the wind of pride). Come with the vanity of your heart, by which you set your sails to winds that were contrary to your salvation. For with the wind of self-esteem, you filled the sail of self-love.'

"In this way you hastened down the stream of the delights and dignities of the world by your own will. You followed your fragile flesh and the temptations of the devil, who, with the sail of your self-love and self-will set, has led you along the underway, which is a running stream, and so has brought you with himself to eternal damnation."

Of the second rebuke of injustice and false judgment, in general and in particular.

"This second rebuke, dearest daughter, is indeed a condemnation, for the soul has arrived at the end, where there can be no remedy. It is at the extremity of death, where it finds the worm of conscience, which I told you was blinded self-love. Now at the time of death, since it cannot get out of my hands, it begins to see, and therefore it is gnawed with remorse that its own sin has brought it into such great evil.

"But if the soul has light to know and grieve for its fault, not on account of the pain of hell that follows upon it, but on account of pain at its offense against me, who am supreme and eternal Good, still it can find mercy. However, if it passes the bridge of death alone and without light, with the worm of conscience and without the hope of the Blood, and bewails itself more on account of its first condemnation than on account of my displeasure, it arrives at eternal damnation.

"Then it is that my justice rebukes the soul cruelly of injustice and of false judgment—not so much of general injustice and false judgment, which it has practiced generally in all its works. No, my rebuke is due much more to the particular injustice and false judgment that it practices at the end, in judging its misery greater than my mercy. This is the sin which is pardoned neither here nor there, because the soul cannot be pardoned, that disparages my mercy. Therefore this last sin is graver to me than all the other sins that the soul has committed. For this reason Judas's despair displeased me more, and was graver to my Son, than his betrayal of him.

"So it is that these are rebuked of their false judgment that their sin is greater than my mercy. On that account, they are punished with the devils and eternally tortured with them.

"And they are rebuked of injustice, because they grieve more over their condemnation than over my displeasure. They do not render to me what is mine, and to themselves what is theirs. For to me, they ought to render love. And to themselves they ought to render bitterness with contrition of heart, and offer it to me for the offense they have done me. But they do the opposite, because to themselves they give love, pitying themselves and grieving on account of the pain they expect for their sin. So you see that they are guilty of injustice and false judgment, and are punished for the one and the other together.

"Because they disparage my mercy, it is with justice that I send them, along with their cruel servant, sensuality, to the cruel tyrant, the devil, whose servants they made themselves through their own sensuality. And I do this so that, together, they are punished and tormented, as together they have offended me. They are tormented, I say, by my ministering devils, whom my judgment has appointed to torment those who have done evil."

Of the glory of the blessed.

"Similarly, the just soul, for whom life ends in the affection of charity and the bonds of love, cannot increase in virtue, time having come to an end. But it can always love with the affection with which it comes to me, and that measure is measured to it. It always desires and loves me, and its desire is not in vain—being hungry, it is satisfied; being satisfied, it is hungry. But the tediousness of satiety and the pain of hunger are far from it.

"In love, the blessed rejoice in my eternal vision, participating in the good that I have in myself, everyone according to the measure of love with which they have come to me. Because they have lived in love of me and of their neighbor, they are united together with general and particular love. They rejoice and exult, participating in each other's good with the affection of love, besides the universal good that they also enjoy together.

"And the blessed rejoice and exult with the angels with whom they are placed, according to their various virtues in the world, being all bound in the bonds of love. Also, they have a special participation with those whom they loved with particular affection in the world. With this affection they grew in grace and virtue. And in the life everlasting they have not lost their love, but have it still, their love being added to the universal good. And those souls rejoice in me, and in the other souls and in the blessed spirits, seeing and tasting in them the beauty and the sweetness of my love. And their desires forever cry out to me for the salvation of the whole world.

"So you see that in those bonds of love in which they finished their life, they go on and remain eternally. They are conformed so entirely to my will that they cannot desire except what I desire, because their free-will is bound in the bond of love in such a way that, time failing them, and, dying in a state of grace, they cannot sin any more.

"These then do not await, with fear, the divine judgment, but with joy. The face of my Son will not seem to them terrible or full of hatred, because they finished their lives in love and affection for me and in good-will towards their neighbor. So it is, then, that the transformation is not in his face, when he comes to judge with my divine majesty, but in the vision of those who will be judged by him. To the damned he will appear with hatred and with justice, and to the saved with love and mercy."

Of the use of temptations, and how every soul in its extremity sees its final place, either of pain or of glory, before it is separated from the body.

"The devil, dearest daughter, is the instrument of my justice to torment the souls who have miserably offended me. And I have set him in this life to tempt and harass my creatures. And I have done this, not for my creatures to be conquered, but that they may conquer, proving their virtue, and receive from me the glory of victory. And no one should fear any battle or temptation of the devil that may come to him, because I have made my creatures strong and have given them strength of will, fortified in the blood of my Son. Neither devil nor creature can move this will, because it is yours, given by me.

"You, therefore, are free agents. As such, you can hold onto your free will or leave it, according as you please. It is a weapon, which, if you place it in the hands of the devil, immediately becomes a knife with which he strikes you and slays you. But if you do not give this knife of your will into the hands of the devil, that is, if you do not consent to his temptations and harassment, you will never be injured by the guilt of sin in any temptation. You will even be fortified by it when the eye of your intellect is opened to see my love, which allowed you to be tempted so as to arrive at virtue, by being tested.

"Now, no one arrives at virtue except through knowledge of self and knowledge of me. Such knowledge is more perfectly acquired in the time of temptation, because then man knows that he is nothing, and is unable to lift off himself the pains and vexations from which he would flee. And he knows me in his will, which is strengthened by my goodness so that it does not yield to these thoughts. He has seen that my love permits these temptations, for the devil is weak, and by himself can do nothing unless I allow him. Through love and not through hatred I let him tempt, so that you may conquer and not be conquered, so that you may come to a perfect knowledge of yourself and of me, and so that virtue may be proved—for it is not proved except by its opposite.

"You see, then, that the devil is my minister to torture the damned in hell, and in this life, to exercise and prove virtue in the soul. Not that it is the intention of the devil to prove virtue in you (for he has no love), but rather to deprive you of it. And this he cannot do if you do not wish it.

"See, then, how great is the foolishness of men in making themselves weak, when I have made them strong, and in putting themselves into the hands of the devil. Know, then, that at the moment of death, having passed their life under the perverse lordship of the devil (not that they were forced to do so, for they cannot be forced, but they voluntarily put themselves into his hands), they await no other judgment than that of their own conscience, and desperately, despairingly, come to eternal damnation. Hell, through their hate, surges up to them in the extremity of death, and before they get there, they take hold of it by means of their lord the devil.

"The righteous, on the other hand, who have lived in charity and died in love, if they have lived perfectly in virtue, are illuminated with the light of faith. With perfect hope in the blood of the Lamb, when the extremity of death comes, they see the good that I have prepared for them and embrace it with the arms of love, holding fast with pressure of love to me, the supreme and eternal Good. And so they taste eternal life before they have left the mortal body, that is, before the soul is separated from the body.

"Others who have lived their lives, and have arrived at the last extremity of death with an ordinary charity (not in that great perfection), embrace my mercy with the same light of faith and hope that those perfect ones had. But, in them, it is imperfect. For, because they were imperfect, they constricted my mercy, although they still counted my mercy greater than their sins.

"However, the wicked sinners do the contrary, for, seeing with desperation their destination, they embrace it with hatred. So it is that neither the one nor the other waits for judgment, but, in departing this life, they receive their place every one of them, and they taste it and possess it before they depart from the body, at the extremity of death. The damned receive their place with hatred and with despair, and the perfect ones with love and the light of faith, and with the hope of the Blood. And the imperfect arrive at the place of Purgatory, with mercy and the same faith."

How the devil gets hold of souls, under pretense
of some good; and, how those are deceived who
keep by the river, and not by the bridge, for, wishing
to flee from pains, they fall into them; and
of the vision of a tree, that this soul once had.

"I have told you that the devil invites men to the water of death, that is, to that which he has, and, blinding them with the pleasures and conditions of the world, he catches them with the hook of pleasure, under the pretense of good. In no other way could he catch them, since they would not allow themselves to be caught if they saw that they would obtain no good or pleasure to themselves by doing so. For the soul, by its nature, always relishes good, though it is true that the soul, blinded by self-love, does not always know and discern what is truly good and profitable to the soul and to the body.

"Therefore the devil, seeing them blinded by self-love, iniquitously places before them various delights, colored so as to have the appearance of some benefit or good. And he gives to everyone according to his condition, and according to the principal vices to which he sees him to be most disposed. He gives delights of one kind to the secular, of another to the religious, and others to prelates and noblemen, according to their different conditions. I have told you this because I will now speak to you of those who drown themselves in the river, and who care for nothing but themselves, loving themselves to my injury. And I will relate to you their end.

"Now I want to show you how they deceive themselves, and how, wishing to flee from troubles, they fall into them. Because it seems to them that following me, that is, walking by the way of the bridge—the Word, my Son—is great toil, they draw back, fearing the thorn. This is because they are blinded and do not know or see the truth, as I showed it to you in the beginning of your life, when you prayed to me to have mercy on the world and to draw it out of the darkness of mortal sin.

"I then showed you myself under the figure of a tree, of which you saw neither the beginning nor the end, so that you did not see that the roots were united with the earth of your humanity. At the foot of the tree there was a certain thorn, from which all those who love their own sensuality kept away, running instead to a mountain of Lolla, in which one figured to oneself all the delights of the world. That Lolla seemed to be of grain but was not, and, therefore, many souls died of hunger on it. And many, recognizing the deceits of the world, returned to the tree and underwent the thorn, which is the deliberation of the will.

"Deliberation of the will, before it is made, is a thorn that appears to man to stand in the way of following the truth. Conscience always fights on one side, and sensuality on the other. But as soon as man, with hatred and displeasure of himself, manfully makes up his mind and saying, 'I wish to follow Christ crucified,' he breaks at once the thorn and finds inestimable sweetness. Some find more and some less, according to their disposition and desire. I said to you, 'I am your God, unmoving and unchangeable, and I do not draw back from any creature who wants to come to me.'

"As for those who did not return to the tree and undergo the thorn, I have shown them the truth: I have made myself visible to them, and I have shown them what it is to love anything without me. But they, as if blinded by the fog of disordinate love, know neither me nor themselves. You see how deceived they are, choosing rather to die of hunger than to undergo a little thorn.

"And they cannot escape enduring pain, for no one can pass through this life without a cross, far less those who travel by the lower way. Not that my servants pass without pain, but their pain is alleviated.

"And because by sin, the world germinates thorns and tribulations, and because this river flows with tempestuous waters, I gave you the bridge so that you might not be drowned.

"I have shown you how they are deceived by a disordinate fear, and how I am your God, immovable, who am not an acceptor of persons but of holy desire. And this I have shown you under the figure of the tree."

How the world germinates thorns, but there are
those whom they do not harm, although no one
passes through this life without pain.

"Now I want to show you to whom the thorns
and tribulations that the world germinated
through sin do harm, and to whom they do not. So
far, I have shown you both the damnation of sinners
and my goodness, and have told you how the
wicked are deceived by their own sensuality. Now I
wish to tell you how it is only they themselves who
are injured by the thorns. No one born passes
through this life without pain, bodily or mental. My
servants bear bodily pain, but their minds are free.
That is, they do not feel the weariness of the pain.
For their will is in agreement with mine, and it is the
will that gives trouble to man. They have pain of
mind and body who taste the pledge of hell while in
this life. But my servants taste the pledge of eternal
life.

"Do you know what is the special good of the
blessed ones? It is having their desire filled with
what they desire. So you see that my servants are
blessed principally in seeing and in knowing me. In
this vision and knowledge their will is fulfilled, for
they have what they desire to have, and so they are
satisfied.

"For this reason I told you that tasting eternal
life consists especially in having what the will

desires, and thus being satisfied. But know that the
will is satisfied in seeing and knowing me. In this life
then, my servants taste the pledge of eternal life.
They taste the things above, with which they will be
satisfied.

"But how do they have the pledge in this present
life? They have it by seeing my goodness in themselves, and by knowing my truth. Their intellect
(which is the eye of the soul), illuminated in me,
possesses my truth. This eye has the pupil of the most
holy faith, the light of which enables the soul to
discern, to know, and to follow the way and the doctrine of my Truth—the Word incarnate. Without this
pupil of faith, the soul would not see, except as one
who has the form of the eye, but who has covered the
pupil (without which the eye cannot see) with a cloth.

"So the pupil of the intellect is faith. If the soul has
covered faith with the cloth of infidelity, drawn over
it by self-love, it does not see. It has only the form of
the eye without the light, because it has hidden the
pupil. Thus you see that in seeing, my servants know,
and in knowing, they love, and in loving, they deny
and lose their self-will. Their own will now lost, they
clothe themselves in my will. And I will nothing but
your sanctification.

"So at once my servants set out, turning their back
on the way below, and begin to ascend by the bridge.
They pass over the thorns, which do not hurt them,
for their feet are shod with the affection of my love. I
told you that my servants suffer corporally but not

mentally, because the sensitive will, which gives pain and afflicts the mind of the creature, is dead. Therefore, since the will is not there, neither is there any pain.

"My servants bear everything with reverence, deeming themselves favored in having tribulation for my sake, and they desire nothing but what I desire. If I allow the devil to trouble them, permitting temptations to prove them in virtue, they resist with their will fortified in me. They humiliate themselves, deeming themselves unworthy of peace and quiet of mind, and deserving of pain. And so they proceed with cheerfulness and self-knowledge, without painful affliction.

"And if tribulations on man's account, or infirmity, or poverty, or a change of worldly condition, or the loss of children or of other much loved creatures (all of which are thorns that the earth produced after sin) come upon them, they endure them all with the light of reason and holy faith. They look to me, who am the supreme Good, and who cannot desire other than good. For that reason I permit these tribulations through love and not through hatred.

"And those who love me recognize this. Examining themselves, they see their sins and understand by the light of faith that good must be rewarded and evil punished. They see that every little sin merits infinite pain, because it is against me, who am infinite Good. Therefore they deem themselves favored, because I punish them in this life, and in this finite time. By their punishment they drive away sin with contrition of heart, and with perfect patience they merit the infinite good with which their labors are rewarded.

"Hereafter they know that all labor in this life is small, because time is short. Time is like the point of a needle and no more, and when time has passed, labor is ended. Therefore you see that the labor is small. They endure with patience, and the thorns they pass through do not touch their heart, because their heart is drawn out of them and united to me by the affection of love.

"It is a quite true, then, that my servants do taste eternal life, receiving the pledge of it in this life. Though they walk on thorns they are not pricked, because they have known my supreme goodness and searched for it where it was to be found, that is in the Word, my only-begotten Son."

How if the three powers of the soul (namely, its intellect, memory, and will) are not united, there cannot be perseverance, without which no one arrives at his end.

"I have explained to you that the three steps of the bridge, which is the body of my only Son, are his feet, his side, and his mouth. I will show you now how those three steps are related to the three powers of the soul, which are its intellect, memory, and will.

Just as no one who wishes to pass by the bridge and doctrine of my truth can mount one without the other, so the soul cannot persevere except by the union of its three powers.

"There are two goals, and, for the attainment of either, perseverance is needful—they are vice and virtue. If you desire to arrive at life, you must persevere in virtue, and if you would have eternal death, you must persevere in vice. Thus it is with perseverance that those who want life arrive at me who am life, and it is with perseverance that those who taste the water of death arrive at the devil."

An exposition on Christ's words: "Whosoever thirsts, let him come to me and drink."

"You were all invited, corporately and individually, by my truth, when he cried in the temple, 'Whosoever thirsts, let him come to me and drink, for I am the fountain of the water of life.' He did not say, 'Go to the Father and drink,' but he said, 'Come to me.' He spoke these words, because in me, the Father, there can be no pain, but in my Son there can be pain. And you, while you are pilgrims and way-farers in this mortal life, cannot be without pain, because the earth, through sin, brought forth thorns.

"And why did my Son say, 'Let him come to me and drink'? Because whoever follows his doctrine, whether in the most perfect way or by dwelling in the life of common charity, finds the water of life to drink by tasting the fruit of the Blood, through the union of the divine nature with the human nature. And you, finding yourselves in him, find yourselves also in me, who am the Sea of Peace, because I am one with him, and he with me. So you are invited to the fountain of living water of grace.

"It is right for you to keep by him who is made for you a bridge, not being turned back by any contrary wind that may arise, whether winds of prosperity or of adversity. And it is right for you to persevere till you find me, who am the giver of the water of life, through this sweet and loving Word, my only-begotten Son.

"Why did my Son say, 'I am the fountain of living water'? Because he was the fountain that contained me, the giver of the living water, through the union of divine and human nature. Why did he say, 'Come to me and drink'? Because you cannot pass through this mortal life without pain. In me, the divine Father, there can be no pain, but in him because of his mortal life there can be pain. Therefore of him I made for you a bridge. No one can come to me except by him, as he told you in the words 'No one can come to the Father except by me.'

"Now you have seen the way to which you should keep, and how you should keep to it, namely with perseverance. Otherwise you shall not drink from the fountain of living water. Only through perseverance can you receive the crown of glory and victory in the life everlasting."

The general method by which every rational creature can come out of the sea of the world, and go to the sea of peace by the holy bridge.

"I will now return to the three steps that you must climb in order to exit from the river without drowning and attain the living water, to which you are invited, and to desire my presence in the midst of you. For on this way which you should follow, I am in your midst, by grace reposing in your souls.

"In order to have the desire to mount the steps, you must be thirsty, because only those who thirst are invited: 'Whoever thirsts, let him come to me and drink.'

"One who is not thirsty will not persevere, for either fatigue will cause him to stop, or pleasure will. A person who is not thirsty does not care to carry the vessel with which he may get water. Neither does he care for the company, and he cannot go alone. So he turns back at the smallest prick of persecution, for he does not love the way. He is afraid because he is alone; if he were accompanied, he would not be afraid. If only he had ascended the three steps he would not have been alone, and would, therefore, have been secure. You must then be thirsty and gather yourselves together, as it is said, 'two or three or more.'

"Why is it said, 'two or three or more'? The number one is excluded, for, unless one has a companion, I cannot be in the midst. This is no indifferent trifle, for one who is wrapped up in self-love is solitary.

"Why is he solitary? Because he is separated from my grace and the love of his neighbor. Being, by sin, deprived of me, he turns to that which is nothing. So a solitary person, that is, one who is alone in self-love, is not mentioned by my Truth and is not acceptable to me. He says, then, 'If there are two or three or more gathered together in my name, I will be in the midst of them.'

"You know that all the commandments of the Law are completely contained in two, and if these two are not observed then the Law is not observed. The two commandments are to love me above everything, and your neighbor as yourself. These two are the beginning, the middle, and the end of the Law.

"These two commandments cannot be gathered together in my name without three, that is without the congregation of the powers of the soul: the memory, the intellect, and the will. The memory retains the remembrance of my benefits and my goodness. The intellect gazes into the inexpressible love that I have shown you by means of my only-begotten Son. I have placed him as the object of the vision of your intellect, so that, in him, you behold the fire of my love. The will drives you to love and desire me, who am your end.

"When these virtues and powers of the soul are congregated together in my name, I am in the midst of them by grace. Then one who is full of my love and love of his neighbor, suddenly finds himself the companion of many royal virtues.

"It is then that the appetite of the soul is disposed to thirst—thirst, I say, for virtue, the honor of my name, and salvation of souls. His every other thirst is spent and dead, and he then proceeds securely without any servile fear, having ascended the first step of the affection. The affection, stripped of self-love, mounts above itself and above transitory things. Or, if he will still hold, he does so according to my will— that is, with a holy and true fear and a love of virtue.

"He then finds that he has attained to the second step—the light of the intellect. This light is, through Christ crucified, mirrored in heartfelt love of me, for through him have I shown my love to man.

"Man finds peace and quiet when the memory is filled with my love. You know that an empty thing resounds when touched, but not so when it is full. So the memory, being filled with the light of the intellect, and the affection, being filled with love, will not resound with disordinate merriment or with impatience when moved by the tribulations or delights of the world, because they are full of me, who am every good.

"Having climbed the three steps, the seeker after God finds that the three powers of the soul have been gathered together by his reason in my name. And his soul, having gathered together the two commandments, that is love of me and of one's neighbor, finds itself accompanied by me, who am its strength and security. It walks safely because I am in the midst of it.

"Then he follows on with anxious desire, thirsting after the way of truth, in which way he finds the fountain of the water of life, through his thirst for my honor and his own salvation and that of his neighbor. For without this thirst he would not be able to arrive at the fountain.

"He walks on, carrying the vessel of the heart, emptied of every affection and disordinate love of the world. But emptied, it is immediately filled with other things, for nothing can remain empty. And, being without disordinate love for transitory things, his heart is filled with love of celestial things, and sweet divine love, with which he arrives at the fountain of the water of life, and passes through the door of Christ crucified, and tastes the water of life, finding himself in me, the Sea of Peace."

*How servile fear is not sufficient, without the
love of virtue, to give eternal life; and how the
laws of fear and of love are united.*

Then the goodness of God, wishing to satisfy the
desire of that servant, said, "Do you see those?
They have arisen with servile fear from the vomit of
mortal sin, but if they do not arise with love of
virtue they will not be given eternal life. Only love
with holy fear is sufficient, because the law is founded
in love and holy fear. The old law was the law of
fear given by me to Moses, and by that law those
who committed sin suffered the penalty of it.

"The new law is the law of love, given by the
word of my only-begotten Son, and is founded in
love alone. The new law does not break the old law,
but rather fulfills it, as said my Truth, 'I come not to
destroy the law, but to fulfill it.' And he united the
law of fear with that of love.

"Through love the imperfection of fear of the
penalty was taken away, and the perfection of holy
fear remained—that is, the fear of offending, not
fear of one's own damnation, but fear of offending
me, who am supreme Good. So the imperfect law
was made perfect with the law of love.

"Therefore, after the fire of my only-begotten
Son came and brought the fire of my charity into
your humanity with abundance of mercy, the penalty

of the sins committed by humanity was taken away. That is, one who offended was no longer punished suddenly, as was of old given and ordained in the law of Moses.

"There is, therefore, no need for servile fear. This does not mean that sin is not punished, but that the punishment is reserved—unless the person punishes himself in this life with perfect contrition. He ought, then, to arise from servile fear, and arrive at love and holy fear of me. Otherwise there is no remedy against his falling back again into the river, and reaching the waters of tribulation, and seeking the thorns of consolation. For all consolations of mortal life are thorns that pierce the soul who loves them disordinately."

How, by ridding oneself of servile fear, which is the state of imperfection, and attaining the first step of the holy bridge, one arrives at the second step, which is the state of perfection.

"I told you that no one could go by the bridge or come out of the river without climbing the three steps, which is the truth. There are some who climb imperfectly, and some perfectly, and some climb with the greatest perfection. The first are those who are moved by servile fear and have climbed so far being imperfectly gathered together. That is to say, the soul, having seen the punishment that follows its sin, climbs and gathers its memory to recollect its vice. With its memory it gathers its intellect to see the punishment it expects to receive for its fault, and its will to move it to hate that fault. Let us consider this to be the first step and the first gathering together of the powers of the soul, which should be exercised by the light of the intellect with the pupil of the eye of holy faith. The eye of holy faith looks not only at the punishment of sin, but at the fruit of virtue, and the love which I bear to the soul, so that it may climb with love and affection and be stripped of servile fear. And doing so, such souls will become faithful and not unfaithful servants, serving me through love and not through fear. And if, with hatred of sin, they employ their minds to dig out the root of their self-love with prudence, constancy, and perseverance, they will succeed in doing so.

"But there are many who begin their course climbing so slowly, and render their debt to me by such small degrees, and with such negligence and ignorance, that they suddenly faint. Every little breeze catches their sails and turns their prow backwards. Consequently, because they climb imperfectly to the first step of the bridge of Christ crucified, they do not arrive at the second step of his heart."

*Of the imperfection of those who love God for
their own profit, delight, and consolation.*

"There are some who have become faithful servants,
serving me faithfully without servile fear of
punishment, but rather with love. This very love, however, is imperfect if they serve me with a view to their
own profit, or the delight and pleasure they find in me.

"Do you know what proves the imperfection of
this love? Towards me their love grows weak when,
on occasion, in order to train them in virtue and
raise them above their imperfection, I withdraw my
consolation from their minds and allow them to fall
into battles and perplexities.

"This I do so that, coming to perfect self-
knowledge, they may know that of themselves they
are nothing and have no grace. Accordingly, in time of
battle they ought to flee to me, as their benefactor,
seeking me alone, with true humility. I withhold from
them the purpose for which I treat them in this
manner, withdrawing from them consolation indeed,
but not grace.

"At such a time these weak ones relax their
energy, impatiently turning backwards. Sometimes
they abandon, under the guise of virtue, many of
their exercises, saying to themselves, 'This labor
does not profit me.' All this they do, because they
feel themselves deprived of mental consolation.

"Such a soul acts imperfectly, for it has not yet unwound the bandage of spiritual self-love, for, had it unwound it it would see that, in truth, everything proceeds from me. No leaf of a tree falls to the ground without my providence. What I give and promise to my creatures, I give and promise to them for their sanctification, which is the good and the end for which I created them.

"My creatures should see and know that I wish nothing but their good, through the blood of my only-begotten Son, in which they are washed from their iniquities. By this blood they are enabled to know how, in order to give them eternal life, I created them in my image and likeness. And I re-created them to grace with the blood of my Son, making them sons of adoption. But, since they are imperfect, they make use of me only for their own profit, relaxing their love for their neighbor.

"Thus, some come to nothing through the fear of enduring pain. Others come to nothing because they slacken their pace and cease to render service to their neighbor. And they withdraw their charity if they see their own profit or consolation withdrawn from them. This happens because their love was originally impure, that is, it was a love based only on desire of their own advantage. If, through a desire for perfection, they do not recognize this imperfection of theirs, it is impossible for them not to turn back.

"For those who desire eternal life, a pure love, detached from themselves, is necessary. For to gain eternal life it is not enough to flee from sin for fear of punishment, or to embrace virtue from the motive of one's own advantage. Sin should be abandoned because it is displeasing to me, and virtue should be loved for my sake.

"It is true that, generally speaking, every person is first called by fear, but this is because the soul itself is at first imperfect. From this imperfection it must advance to perfection. And it must do so while it lives, by a generous love to me with a pure and virtuous heart that takes no thought for itself. Or, at least, it must do so in the moment of death, recognizing its own imperfection, and having the purpose, if it but had time, of serving me, irrespective of itself.

"It was with this imperfect love that St. Peter loved the sweet and good Jesus, my only-begotten Son, and enjoyed most pleasantly his sweet conversation. But when the time of trouble came, he failed. So disgraceful was his fall, that, not only could he not bear any pain himself, but his terror of the very approach of pain caused him to fall and deny the Lord, with the words, 'I have never known him.'

"The soul who has climbed this step with servile fear and mercenary love alone, falls into many troubles. Such souls should arise and become my children, and serve me, irrespective of themselves. For I, who am the rewarder of every labor, render to each man according to his state and his labor.

"If these souls do not abandon the practice of holy prayer and other good works, but go on, with perseverance, to increase their virtues, they will arrive at the state of filial love. I respond to them with the same love with which they love me, so that, if they love me as a servant does his master, I pay them their wages according to what they deserve. But I do not reveal myself to them, because secrets are revealed to a friend, and not to a servant.

"Yet it is true, that a servant may so advance by the virtuous love that he bears to his master, as to become a very dear friend. And this is the case of some of these of whom I have spoken. But while they remain in the state of mercenary love, I do not manifest myself to them.

"If these, through displeasure at their imperfection and love of virtue, dig up, with hatred, the root of spiritual self-love, and mount to the throne of conscience, reasoning with themselves so as to quell the motions of servile fear in their heart and to correct mercenary love by the light of the holy faith, they will be so pleasing to me that they will attain to the love of a friend. And I will manifest myself to them, as my Truth said in these words: 'He who loves me shall be one with me and I with him, and I will manifest myself to him and we will dwell together.'

"This is the state of two dear friends, for though they are two in body, yet they are one in soul through the affection of love, because love transforms the lover into the object loved. And where two friends have one soul, there can be no secret between them. That is why my Truth said: 'I will come and we will dwell together,' and this is the truth."

Of the way in which God manifests
himself to the soul who loves him.

"Do you know how I manifest myself to the soul who loves me in truth, and follows the doctrine of my sweet and loving Word?

"In many my virtue is manifested in the soul in proportion to its desire. But I also make three special manifestations. The first manifestation of my virtue, that is, of my love and charity in the soul, is made through the word of my Son and shown in the blood that he spilled with such fire of love.

"Now this charity is manifested in two ways: first, in general, to ordinary people, that is to those who live in the ordinary grace of God. It is manifested to them by the many and diverse benefits that they receive from me.

"The second mode of manifestation, which is developed from the first, is peculiar to those who have become my friends in the way mentioned above. It is known through a sentiment of the soul, by which they taste, know, prove, and feel it.

"This second manifestation, however, is in men themselves: They manifest me through the affection of their love. For though I am no acceptor of creatures,

I am an acceptor of holy desires, and find myself in the soul according to the precise degree of perfection that it seeks in me.

"Sometimes I manifest myself (and this is also a part of the second manifestation) by endowing men with the spirit of prophecy, showing them the things of the future. This I do in various ways, according to the need I see in the soul itself and in other creatures.

"At other times the third manifestation takes place. I then form in the mind the presence of the Truth, my only-begotten Son, in many ways, according to the will and the desire of the soul. Sometimes it seeks me in prayer, wishing to know my power, and I satisfy it by causing it to taste and see my virtue. Sometimes it seeks me in the wisdom of my Son, and I satisfy it by placing his wisdom before the eye of its intellect, sometimes in the clemency of the Holy Spirit. And then my goodness causes it to taste the fire of divine charity, and to conceive the true and royal virtues, which are founded on the pure love of one's neighbor."

How the soul, after having mounted the first step of the bridge, should proceed to mount the second.

"You have now seen how excellent is the state of one who has attained to the love of a friend. Climbing with the foot of affection, he has reached the secret of the heart, which is the second of the three steps figured in the body of my Son. I wish to show you how one becomes a friend and how, from a friend, he grows into a son, attaining to filial love, and how one may know if he has become a friend.

"In the beginning, a man serves me imperfectly through servile fear. But by practice and perseverance, he arrives at the love of delight, finding his own delight and profit in me. This is a necessary stage, through which he must pass, to attain perfect love. I call filial love perfect, because by it, a man receives his inheritance from me, the eternal Father, and because a son's love includes that of a friend, which is why I told you that a friend grows into a son.

"What means does he use to arrive at that state? I will tell you. Every perfection and every virtue proceeds from charity, and charity is nourished by humility, which results from the knowledge and holy hatred of self, that is, sensuality. To arrive at that state, a man must persevere and remain in the cellar of self-knowledge. There he will learn my mercy, through the blood of my only-begotten Son, and will draw to himself this love and my divine charity. As he does so, he will extirpate his perverse self-will, both spiritual and temporal.

"In this process he will find himself hiding in his own house, as did Peter, who, after the sin of denying my Son, began to weep. Yet Peter's lamentations were imperfect, and they remained so until after the forty days, that is until after the Ascension.

"When my Truth returned to me, in his humanity, Peter and the others concealed themselves in the house, awaiting the coming of the Holy Spirit whom my Truth had promised them. They remained barred in from fear, because the soul always fears until it arrives at true love. But they persevered in fasting and in humble and continual prayer until they received the abundance of the Holy Spirit. Then they lost their fear, and followed and preached Christ crucified.

"The soul who wishes to arrive at this perfection, after it has risen from the guilt of mortal sin, recognizing it for what it is, begins to weep from fear of the penalty for its sin. Then it rises to the consideration of my mercy, in which contemplation it finds its own pleasure and profit. This is an imperfect state, and I, in order to develop perfection in the soul, after the 'forty days,' that is after these two states, withdraw myself from time to time, not in grace but in feeling. My Truth showed you this when he said to the disciples, 'I will go and will return to you.'

"Everything that he said was said primarily and in particular to the disciples. But his sayings also referred in general to the whole present and future, that is, to those who should come after. He said, 'I will go and will return to you'; and so it was. For, when the Holy Spirit returned upon the disciples, he did not return alone, but came with my power and the wisdom of the Son, who is one with me. And he came his own clemency, which proceeds from me, the Father, and from the Son.

"Now, as I told you, in order to raise the soul from imperfection, I withdraw myself from its sentiment, depriving it of former consolations. When it was in the guilt of mortal sin, it had separated itself from me. At that time I deprived it of grace through its own guilt, because that guilt had barred the door of its desires. Therefore the sun of grace did not shine, not through its own defect, but through the defect of the creature, who bars the door of desire. When the soul knows itself and its darkness, it opens the window and vomits its filth, by holy confession.

"Then I, having returned to the soul by grace, withdraw myself from it by sentiment. And this I do in order to humble it, and to cause it to seek me in truth, and to prove it in the light of faith, so that it may come to prudence. Then, if it loves me without thought of self and with lively faith and with hatred of its own sensuality, it rejoices in the time of trouble, deeming itself unworthy of peace and quietness of mind.

"Now comes the second of the three things of which I spoke, that is: how the soul arrives at perfection, and what it does when it is perfect. This is what it does. Though it perceives that I have withdrawn myself, it does not, on that account, look back. Rather, it perseveres with humility in its practices, remaining barred in the house of self-knowledge.

"And continuing to dwell in that house, the soul awaits, with lively faith, the coming of the Holy Spirit—that is of me, who am the fire of charity.

How does the soul await me? Not in idleness, but in watching and continued prayer. And not only does it wait with physical, but also with intellectual watching, that is, with the eye of its mind alert and watching with the light of faith. It extirpates, with hatred, the wandering thoughts of its heart, looking for the affection of my charity and knowing that I desire nothing but the sanctification, that is certified to it in the blood of my Son.

"As long as the soul's eye watches in this manner, illumined by the knowledge of me and of itself, it continues to pray with the prayer of holy desire, which is a continued prayer. And it also prays with actual prayer, which it practices at the appointed times, according to the orders of the holy church.

"This is what the soul does in order to rise from imperfection and arrive at perfection. And it is to this end, namely that the soul may arrive at perfection, that I withdraw from it, not by grace but by sentiment.

"Once more I leave the soul, so that it may see and know its defects. And this I do so that, feeling itself deprived of consolation and afflicted by pain, it may recognize its own weakness and learn how incapable it is of stability or perseverance, thus cutting down to the very root of spiritual self-love. This should be the end and purpose of all the soul's self-knowledge: to rise above itself, mounting the throne of conscience and not permitting the sentiment of imperfect love to turn again in its death-struggle.

Rather, with correction and reproof, it must dig up the root of self-love with the knife of self-hatred and the love of virtue."

How an imperfect lover of God loves his neighbor also imperfectly, and of the signs of this imperfect love.

"And I would have you know that just as every imperfection and perfection is acquired from me, so is it manifested by means of one's neighbor. And simple souls, who often love creatures with spiritual love, know this well, for, if they have received my love sincerely without any self-regarding considerations, they satisfy the thirst of their love for their neighbor equally sincerely. If a man carries away the vessel that he has filled at the fountain and then drinks of it, the vessel becomes empty. But if he keeps his vessel standing in the fountain while he drinks, it always remains full. So the love of one's neighbor, whether spiritual or temporal, should be drunk in me, without any self-regarding considerations.

"I require that you should love me with the same love with which I love you. This indeed you cannot do, because I loved you without being loved. All the love that you have for me you owe to me, so it is not of grace that you love me, but because you ought to do so. But I love you of grace, and not because I owe you my love.

"To me, in person, you cannot repay the love that I require of you. Therefore I have placed you in the midst of your fellows, so that you may do to them that which you cannot do to me. That is, I give you the opportunity to love your neighbor of free grace, without expecting any return from him. And what you do to him, I count as done to me. This love must be sincere, because with the same love with which you love me, you must love your neighbor.

"Do you know how the imperfection of spiritual love for the creature is shown? It is shown when the lover feels pain if it appears to him that the object of his love does not satisfy or return his love, or when he sees the beloved one's conversation turned aside from him. It is shown when the lover feels himself deprived of consolation, or sees another loved more than he.

"In these and in many other ways it can be seen that the lover's neighborly love is still imperfect, and that, though his love was originally drawn from me, the fountain of all love, he took the vessel out of the water in order to drink from it. It is because his love for me is still imperfect that his neighborly love is so weak, and because the root of self-love has not been properly dug out.

"I often permit such a love to exist so that the soul may in this way come to the knowledge of its own imperfection. And for the same reason I withdraw myself from the soul by sentiment. And this I do so that it may be led to enclose itself in the house of self-knowledge, where every perfection is acquired.

"After this I return into it with more light and with more knowledge of my truth, in proportion to the degree in which it refers to grace the power of slaying its own will. And it never ceases to cultivate the vine of its soul, and to root out the thorns of evil thoughts. These it replaces with the stones of virtues, cemented together in the blood of Christ crucified, which it has found on its journey across the bridge of Christ, my only-begotten Son. For upon the bridge, that is, upon the doctrine of my Truth, the stones were built up, based upon the virtue of his blood. For it is in virtue of this blood that the virtues give life."

A TREATISE OF PRAYER

Of the means that the soul takes to arrive at pure and generous love; here begins the Treatise of Prayer.

"When the soul has passed through the doctrine of Christ crucified, with true love of virtue and hatred of vice, and has arrived at the house of self-knowledge and entered into it, it remains, with its door barred, in watching and constant prayer, separated entirely from the consolations of the world. Why does it shut itself in this manner? It does so out of fear, knowing its own imperfections, and also from the desire of arriving at pure and generous love.

"And because the soul sees and knows well that in no other way can it arrive arrive at pure love, with a lively faith it waits for my arrival, through the increase of grace in it.

"How is a lively faith to be recognized? By perseverance in virtue, and by the fact that the soul never turns back for anything, whatever it may be, nor rises from holy prayer for any reason except

(note well) for obedience or charity's sake. For no
other reason ought the soul to leave off prayer.

"For, during the time ordained for prayer, the
devil is apt to arrive in the soul, causing much more
conflict and trouble than when the soul is not occu-
pied in prayer. This he does so that holy prayer may
become tedious to the soul. He tempts the soul often
with these words: 'This prayer avails you nothing,
for you need attend to nothing except your vocal
prayers.' He does this so that, becoming wearied and
confused in mind, the soul may abandon the practice
of prayer. For prayer is a weapon with which the
soul can defend itself from every adversary, if it is
grasped with the hand of love, by the arm of free
choice in the light of the holy faith."

Here, concerning the sacrament of the body
of Christ, the complete doctrine is given; and
how the soul proceeds from vocal to mental
prayer; and a vision is related which this
devout servant of God once received.

"Know, dearest daughter, how, by humble, continual,
and faithful prayer, with time and perseverance
the soul acquires every virtue. It should persevere and
never abandon prayer, either through the illusion of
the devil or its own fragility. That is, it should never
abandon prayer either on account of any thought or

movement coming from its own body, or on account of the words of any creature. The devil often places himself upon the tongues of creatures, causing them to chatter nonsensically, with the purpose of preventing the prayer of the soul. All of this the soul should pass by, by means of the virtue of perseverance.

"Oh, how sweet and pleasant to that soul and to me is holy prayer, made in the house of knowledge of self and of me. It opens the eye of the intellect to the light of faith and the affections to the abundance of my charity. And my charity was made visible to you through my visible, only-begotten Son, who showed it to you with his blood! This blood intoxicates the soul and clothes it with the fire of divine charity, giving it the food of the sacrament which is placed in the inn of the mystical body of the holy church. That is, the food of the body and blood of my Son, wholly God and wholly man, is administered to you by the hand of my vicar, who holds the key of the blood.

"This is the inn that I mentioned to you, the inn that stands on the bridge to provide food and comfort for the travelers and the pilgrims who pass by the way of the doctrine of my Truth, so they should not faint through weakness.

"This food strengthens little or much according to the desire of the recipient, whether he receives the food sacramentally or virtually. He receives the food sacramentally when he actually communicates with the blessed sacrament. He receives it virtually when he communicates, both by desire for communion and by contemplation of the blood of Christ crucified. It is as if he communicated sacramentally, with the affection of love. For love is to be tasted in the blood, which, as the soul sees, was shed through love. On seeing this the soul becomes intoxicated, and blazes with holy desire and satisfies itself, becoming full of love for me and for its neighbor.

"Where can this love be acquired? In the house of self-knowledge with holy prayer. There, imperfections are lost, even as Peter and the disciples, while they remained in watching and prayer, lost their imperfection and acquired perfection. By what means is this love acquired? By perseverance seasoned with the most holy faith.

"But do not think that the soul receives such ardor and nourishment from prayer if it prays only vocally, as do many souls whose prayers are words rather than love. Such as these give heed to nothing except to completing psalms and saying many Our Fathers. And once they have completed their appointed tale, they do not appear to think of anything further, but seem to place devout attention and love in mere vocal recitation. But the soul is not required to do this, for, in doing only this, it bears but little fruit, which pleases me but little.

"But if you asked me whether the soul should abandon vocal prayer, since it does not seem to everyone that they are called to mental prayer, I would reply 'No.' The soul should advance by degrees, and I know well that, just as the soul is at first imperfect and afterwards perfect, so also is it with its prayer. It should nevertheless continue in vocal prayer, while it is yet imperfect, so as not to fall into idleness.

"But the soul should not say its vocal prayers without joining them to mental prayer. That is, while the soul is reciting vocal prayers, it should endeavor to elevate its mind in my love, with the consideration of its own defects and of the blood of my only-begotten Son. For in the Blood, it finds the breadth of my charity and the remission of its sins.

"And this the soul should do, so that self-knowledge and the consideration of its own defects should make it recognize my goodness in itself and continue its practices with true humility. I do not wish defects to be considered in particular, but in general, so that the mind may not be contaminated by the remembrance of particular and hideous sins.

"But I do not wish the soul to consider its sins, either in general or in particular, without also remembering the blood and the broadness of my mercy, for fear that otherwise it should be brought to confusion. And together with confusion would come the devil, who has caused it, under the banner of contrition and displeasure of sin. And so it would arrive at eternal damnation, not only because of its confusion, but also through the despair that would come to it, because it did not seize the arm of my mercy. This is one of the subtle devices with which the devil deludes my servants.

"In order to escape from the devil's deceit and to be pleasing to me, you must enlarge your hearts and affections in my boundless mercy, with true humility. You know that the pride of the devil cannot resist the humble mind, nor can any confusion of spirit be greater than the broadness of my good mercy, if the soul will only truly hope in my mercy

"Once, if you remember rightly, when the devil wished to overthrow you by confusion, wishing to prove to you that your life had been deluded and that you had not followed my will, you did your duty, which my goodness (which is never withheld from one who will receive it) gave you strength to do. You rose, humbly trusting in my mercy, and saying: 'I confess to my creator that my life has indeed been passed in darkness. But I will hide myself in the wounds of Christ crucified, and bathe myself in his blood. And so shall my iniquities be consumed, and with desire will I rejoice in my creator.'

"You remember that then the devil fled. And, turning round to the opposite side, he endeavored to inflate you with pride, saying: 'You are perfect and pleasing to God, and there is no more need for you to afflict yourself or to lament your sins.' And once more I gave you the light to see your true path, namely, humiliation of yourself.

"And you answered the devil with these words: 'Wretch that I am, John the Baptist never sinned and was sanctified in his mother's womb. And I have committed so many sins, and have hardly begun to know them with grief and true contrition. For I see who God is, who is offended by me, and who I am, who offend him.'

"Then the devil, not being able to resist your humble hope in my goodness, said to you: 'Cursed that you are, for I can find no way to take you. If I put you down through confusion, you rise to heaven on the wings of mercy, and if I raise you on high, you humble yourself down to hell. And when I go into hell you persecute me, so that I will return to you no more, because you strike me with the stick of charity.'

"The soul, therefore, should season the knowledge of itself with the knowledge of my goodness, and then vocal prayer will be of use to the soul who prays it, and pleasing to me. And from the vocal imperfect prayer, practiced with perseverance, the soul will arrive at perfect mental prayer. But if it simply aims at completing its tale, and, preferring vocal prayer it abandons mental prayer, it will never arrive at it.

"Sometimes the soul will be so ignorant that, having resolved to say so many prayers vocally in order to complete its tale will abandon my visitation that it feels by conscience, rather than abandon what it had begun. For I visit its mind sometimes in one way, and sometimes in another. Sometimes I visit it in a flash of self-knowledge or of contrition for sin, sometimes in the broadness of my charity. Sometimes I place before its mind, in various ways, according to my pleasure and the desire of the soul, the presence of my Truth.

"The soul should not abandon my visitation, for, in doing so, it yields to a deception of the devil. The moment it feels its mind disposed by my visitation in the many ways I have told you, it should abandon vocal prayer. Then, once my visitation has passed, if there is time it can resume the vocal prayers it resolved to say. But if it does not have time to complete them, it ought not on that account to be troubled or to suffer annoyance and confusion of mind.

"Of course I am not referring to the Divine Office, which clerics and religious are bound and obliged to say under penalty of offending me, for they must, until death, say their office. But if they, at the hour appointed for saying it, should feel their minds drawn and raised by desire, they should arrange so as to say the office before or after my visitation. Thus they will assure that the debt of rendering the office is not omitted.

"But in any other case, vocal prayer should be abandoned immediately for my visitation. Vocal prayer, made in the way that I have told you, will enable the soul to arrive at perfection. Therefore the soul should not abandon it, but use it in the way that I have told you.

"And so, with practice in perseverance, the soul will in truth taste prayer, and the food of the blood of my only-begotten Son. Therefore I told you that some communicate virtually with the body and blood of Christ, although not sacramentally. That is, they communicate in the affection of charity, which they taste by means of holy prayer. They communicate little or much, according to the affection with which they pray. Those who proceed with little prudence and without method, taste little, and those who proceed with much, taste much.

"For the more the soul tries to loosen its affection from itself and fasten it in me with the light of the intellect, the more it knows. And the more the soul knows, the more it loves. And, loving much, it tastes much.

"You see then, that perfect prayer is not arrived at through many words, but through affection of desire, when the soul raises itself to me, knowing itself and my mercy, seasoned the one with the other. Thus the soul will practice mental and vocal prayer together, for, even as the active and contemplative life are one, so are they.

"Now, vocal or mental prayer can be understood in many different ways. For I have told you that a holy desire is a continual prayer, in the sense that a good and holy will disposes itself with desire to the occasion actually appointed for prayer, in addition to the continual prayer of holy desire. Therefore vocal prayer will be made at the appointed time by the soul who remains firm in a habitual holy will. And sometimes vocal prayer will be continued beyond the appointed time. The length of time will vary according as charity commands for the salvation of one's neighbor, if the soul sees him in need. And it will also vary according to the soul's own needs, which depend on the state in which I have placed her.

"Each person, according to his condition, ought to exert himself for the salvation of souls. For this exercise lies at the root of a holy will. Whatever he may contribute, by words or deeds, towards the salvation of his neighbor, is virtually a prayer. But keep in mind that it does not replace a prayer which one should make oneself at the appointed season.

"As my glorious standard-bearer Paul said, 'He who ceases not to work ceases not to pray.' It was for this reason that I told you that prayer is made in many ways. That is, actual prayer may be united with mental prayer if it is made with the affection of charity, for charity is itself continual prayer.

"I have now told you how mental prayer is reached by exercise and perseverance, and by leaving off vocal prayer in favor of mental, when I visit the soul. I have also spoken to you of common prayer, that is, of vocal prayer in general, made outside of ordained times. And I have spoken to you of the prayers of good-will, and how every exercise, whether performed in oneself or in one's neighbor, with good-will, is prayer. The enclosed soul should therefore spur itself on with prayer. And when it has arrived at friendly and filial love, it does so. Unless the soul keeps to this path, it will always remain tepid and imperfect, and will love me and its neighbor only in proportion to the pleasure it finds in my service."

Of the method by which the soul separates itself from imperfect love, and attains to perfect love, friendly and filial.

"Until now I have shown you in many ways how the soul raises itself from imperfection and attains to perfection. And this it does after it has attained to friendly and filial love. I tell you that it arrives at perfect love by means of perseverance, barring itself into the house of self-knowledge.

"Now, knowledge of self must be seasoned with knowledge of me, lest it bring the soul to confusion. For self-knowledge would cause the soul to hate its own sensitive pleasure and the delight of its own consolations. But from this hatred, founded in humility, it will draw patience. With patience it will become strong against the attacks of the devil, against the persecutions of man, and towards me, when, for its good, I withdraw delight from its mind.

"And if the soul's sensuality, through malevolence, should lift its head against reason, the judgment of conscience will rise against it. With hatred of it, the judgment of conscience will hold out reason against it, not allowing such evil emotions to get by it.

"However, sometimes the soul who lives in holy hatred corrects and rebukes itself, not only for the things that are against reason, but also for things that in reality come from me. This is what my sweet servant St. Gregory meant when he said that a holy and pure conscience makes sin where there is no sin. That is, through purity of conscience the soul sees sin where there is no sin.

"Now the soul who wishes to rise above imperfection should await my providence in the house of self-knowledge, with the light of faith, as did the disciples. For the disciples remained in the house in perseverance, in watching, and in humble and continual prayer, awaiting the coming of the Holy Spirit. The soul should remain fasting and watching, with the eye of its intellect fastened on the doctrine of my truth. And it will become humble because it will know itself in humble and continual prayer, and in holy and true desire."

Of the signs by which the soul knows it has arrived at perfect love.

"It now remains to tell you how it can be seen that souls have arrived at perfect love: by the same sign that was given to the holy disciples after they received the Holy Spirit. At that time they came forth from the house and fearlessly announced the doctrine of my Word, my only-begotten Son, not fearing pain, but rather glorying in it. They did not mind going before the tyrants of the world, to announce the truth to them for the glory and praise of my name.

"So the soul who has awaited me in self-knowledge receives me, on my return to it, with the fire of charity. In charity, while still remaining in the house with perseverance, it conceives the virtues by affection of love and participates in my power.

"With my power and these virtues, this soul overrules and conquers its own sensitive passions, and through charity it participates in the wisdom of my Son. In wisdom it sees and knows my truth, with the eye of its intellect. And it knows the deceptions of spiritual self-love, that is, the imperfect love of its own consolations. It also knows the malice and deceit of the devil, which he practices on those souls who are bound by that imperfect love.

"Therefore this soul arises with hatred of that imperfection and with love of perfection. And, through this love, which is of the Holy Spirit, it participates in his will, fortifying itself to be willing to suffer pain. Then, coming out of the house through my name, it brings forth the virtues on its neighbor.

"Not that by coming out to bring forth the virtues, I mean that the soul leaves the house of self-knowledge. Rather, in the time of its neighbor's need it loses the fear of being deprived of its own consolations, and so it sets out to give birth to those virtues that it has conceived through affection of love.

"The souls who have come forth in this manner have reached the fourth state, which is that of perfect union with me. The two last-mentioned states are united, that is, the one cannot exist without the other. For there cannot be love of me without love of one's neighbor, nor love of the neighbor without love of me."

*How worldly people render glory and praise
to God, whether they want to or not.*

"And so perfect is the soul's vision that it sees the glory and praise of my name, not so much in the angelic nature as in the human. For whether worldly people want to or not, they render glory and praise to my name. Not that they do so in the way they should, loving me above everything, but my mercy shines in them, in the abundance of my charity. I give them time, and I do not order the earth to open and swallow them up on account of their sins. I even wait for them, and command the earth to give them of its fruits, the sun to give them light and warmth, and the sky to move above them. And in all things created and made for them, I use my charity and mercy, with-drawing neither on account of their sins.

"I even give equally to the sinner and to the righteous man, and often more to the sinner than to the righteous man. For the righteous man is able to endure privation, and I take from him the goods of the world that he may the more abundantly enjoy the goods of heaven. So in worldly men my mercy and charity shine, and they render praise and glory to my name even when they persecute my servants. For they prove in my servants the virtues of patience and charity, causing them to suffer humbly and to offer me their persecutions and injuries, thus turning them into my praise and glory.

"So that, whether they want to or not, worldly people render praise and glory to my name, when they intend to do me infamy and wrong."

How even the devils render glory
and praise to God.

"Sinners, such as those of whom I have just spoken, are placed in this life in order to augment the virtues in my servants. In the same way the devils are in hell to serve as my instruments of justice towards the damned. They also serve to augment my glory in my creatures, who are wayfarers and pilgrims on their journey to reach me, their end.

"The devils augment the virtues in my creatures in various ways, exercising them with many temptations and vexations and causing them to injure one another and to take one another's property. This they do, not for the motive of making them receive injury or be deprived of their property, but only to deprive them of charity. But in thinking to deprive my servants, the sinners and devils strengthen them, proving in them the virtues of patience, fortitude, and perseverance. In this way, the devils render praise and glory to my name, and my truth is fulfilled in them.

"Now, my truth created the devils for the praise and glory of me, the eternal Father, and so that they might participate in my beauty. But, rebelling against me in their pride, they fell and lost their vision of me. Therefore they did not render to me glory through the affection of love.

"So I, eternal Truth, have placed the devils as instruments to exercise my servants in virtue in this life and as judicial officers to those who go, for their sins, to the pains of Purgatory. So you see that my truth is fulfilled in them, that is, in that they render me glory, not as citizens of life eternal, of which they are deprived by their sins, but as my officers. As such they manifest justice upon the damned, and upon those in Purgatory."

How the soul, after it has passed through this life, sees fully the praise and glory of my name in everything, and though in it the pain of desire is ended, the desire itself is not.

"Thus in all things created—in all rational creatures and in all devils—is seen the glory and praise of my name. Who can see it? The soul who has left the body and has reached me, its end, sees it clearly, and, in seeing, knows the truth. Seeing me, the eternal Father, it loves. And loving, it is satisfied. Satisfied, it knows the truth, and its will is stayed in my will, bound and made stable. Therefore in nothing can it suffer pain, because it has what it desired to have before it saw me, namely, the glory and praise of my name.

"So now, in truth, this soul sees my glory completely in my saints, in the blessed spirits, and in all creatures and things, even in the devils. And although it also sees the injury done to me, which before caused it sorrow, the injury no longer now can give it pain, but only compassion. And this is because it loves without pain, and prays to me continually, with affection of love, that I will have mercy on the world.

"Pain in this soul is ended, but not love, just as the tortured desire which my Word, the Son, had borne from the beginning when I sent him into the world, ended on the cross in his painful death—but not his love. For if the love that I showed you by means of my Son had terminated and ended then, you would not exist, because by love you are made. And if my love had been drawn back, you could not exist. My love created you, and my love possesses you, because I am one with my Truth, and he, the Word incarnate, is one with me.

"You see then, that the saints and every soul in eternal life desire the salvation of souls without pain, because pain ended in their death, but not so the affection of love.

"Thus, as if intoxicated with the blood of the immaculate Lamb and clothed in the love of their neighbor, they pass through the narrow gate. There, bathed in the blood of Christ crucified, they find themselves in me, the Sea of Peace. Raised from imperfection, far from satiety, they have arrived at perfection, and are satisfied by every good."

*How the soul who finds itself in the unitive state
desires infinitely to unite itself to God.*

"When I depart from the soul so that the body may return a little to its bodily sentiment, the soul, on account of the union that it had made with me, is impatient in its life. It becomes tired of being deprived of union with me and the conversation of the immortals who render glory to me. And it grows weary of finding itself amid the conversation of mortals, and of seeing them so miserably offending me.

"This vision of offenses against me is the torture that such souls always have. And that torture, along with the desire to see me, renders their life intolerable to them. Nevertheless, as their will is not their own, but becomes one with mine, they cannot desire other than what I desire. Though they desire to come and be with me, they are content to remain with their pain, if I desire them to remain, for the greater praise and glory of my name and the salvation of souls. So in nothing are these souls in discord with my will, but they run their course with ecstatic desire, clothed in Christ crucified, and keeping by the bridge of his doctrine, glorying in his shame and pains.

"As much as these souls appear to be suffering, they are rejoicing, because enduring many tribulations is to them a relief in the desire that they have for death. For oftentimes their desire and their will to suffer pain mitigates the pain caused them by their desire to leave the body.

"These who are in the third state not only endure with patience, but they glory, through my name, in bearing much tribulation. In bearing tribulation they find pleasure, and when I permit to them many tribulations they rejoice, seeing themselves clothed with the suffering and shame of Christ crucified.

"Therefore if it were possible for these souls to have virtue without toil, they would not want it. They would rather delight in the Cross, with Christ, acquiring virtue with pain, than to obtain eternal life in any other way. Why? Because they are inflamed and steeped in the Blood, where they find the blaze of my charity. For my charity is a fire proceeding from me, ravishing their heart and mind and making their sacrifices acceptable.

"Thus, when the affection behind the intellect is nourished and united with me, the eye of the intellect is lifted up and gazes into my deity. This is a sight that I grant to the soul, infused with grace, who, in truth, loves and serves me."

How those, who have arrived at the unitive
state have the eye of their intellect illuminated
by supernatural light, infused by grace. And
how it is better to go for counsel, for the salvation
of the soul, to a humble and holy conscience
than to a proud man of letters.

"With this light that is given to the eye of the intellect, Thomas Aquinas saw me, and for that reason he acquired the light of much knowledge. Augustine, Jerome, the teachers of the church, and my saints were illuminated by my truth to know and understand my truth in the midst of darkness.

"By my truth I mean the Holy Scripture, which seemed dark because it was not understood. And this was not through any defect of the Scriptures, but of those who heard them and did not understand them. Therefore I sent the light of the Holy Scripture to illuminate men's blind and coarse understanding, and to lift up the eye of their intellect to know the truth. And I, Fire, Acceptor of sacrifices, ravishing away from them their darkness, give them light.

"This was not a natural light, but a supernatural one, so that, though in darkness, men might know the truth. So you see that the eye of the intellect has received supernatural light, infused by grace, by which the teachers and saints knew light in darkness. And of darkness they made light.

"The intellect existed before the Scriptures were formed. Therefore from the intellect came knowledge, because in seeing, they discerned. It was in this way that the holy prophets and fathers understood, they who prophesied of the coming and death of my Son. And it was in this way that the apostles understood, after the coming of the Holy Spirit, who gave them that supernatural light. The evangelists, doctors, professors, virgins, and martyrs were all likewise illuminated by that perfect light. And everyone has had the illumination of this light as he needed it for his salvation or that of others, or for the exposition of the Scriptures.

"The teachers of the holy knowledge had it as they expounded on the doctrine of my truth, the preaching of the apostles, and the Gospels of the evangelists. The martyrs had it, declaring in their blood the most holy faith, the fruit and the treasure of the blood of the Lamb. The virgins had it in the affection of charity and purity.

"To the obedient ones is declared, by this light, the obedience of the Word, showing them the perfection of obedience, which shines in my Truth. And my Truth, for the obedience that I imposed upon him, ran to the opprobrious death of the cross.

"This light is to be seen in the Old and New Testaments. In the Old, by it the prophecies of the holy prophets were seen by the eye of the intellect, and known. In the New Testament of the evangelical life, how is the gospel declared to the faithful? By this same light.

"And because the New Testament proceeded from the same light, the new law did not break the old law. Rather, the two laws are bound together. The imperfection of the old law, founded in fear alone, was taken from it by the coming of the Word of my only-begotten Son with the law of love. He completed the old law by giving it love, and replaced the fear of penalty by holy fear. And, to show that he was not a breaker of laws my Truth said to the disciples: 'I came not to dissolve the law, but to fulfill it.'

"It is almost as if my Truth would say to them— The law is now imperfect, but with my blood I will make it perfect, and I will fill it up with what it lacks. I will take away the fear of penalty and found it on love and holy fear. How was this declared to be the truth? By this same supernatural light, which was and is given by grace to all.

"Now, who will receive this light? Every light that comes from holy Scripture comes and came from this supernatural light. Ignorant and proud men of science were blind notwithstanding this light, because their pride and the cloud of self-love covered up and put out the light. For that reason they understood the holy Scripture literally rather than with understanding, and tasted only the letter of it, still desiring many other books.

"Such men do not get to the heart of the Scripture, because they have deprived themselves of the light with which the Scripture is found and expounded. They are annoyed and they murmur, because they find much in Scripture that appears to them gross and idiotic.

"Nevertheless, such men appear to be much enlightened in their knowledge of Scripture, as if they had studied it for long. This is not remarkable, because of course they have the natural light whence proceeds science. But because they have lost the supernatural light, infused by grace, they neither see nor know my goodness, nor the grace of my servants.

"Therefore, I say to you, it is much better to go for counsel for the salvation of the soul, to a person of holy and upright conscience, than to a proud man of letters who has learned much knowledge. Such a one can only offer what he has himself, and, because of his darkness, it may appear to you that, from what he says, the Scriptures offer darkness. You will find the opposite with my servants, because they offer the light that is in them, with hunger and desire for the soul's salvation.

"This I have told you, my sweetest daughter, that you might know the perfection of this union-producing state, when the eye of the intellect is ravished by the fire of my charity, in which it receives the supernatural light. With this light the souls in the state of union love me, because love follows the intellect, and the more it knows the more it can love. So the one feeds the other, and, with this light, they both arrive at the eternal vision of me, in which vision they see and taste me, in truth.

"At that point the soul becomes separated from the body, as I told you when I spoke to you of the blissfulness that the soul receives in me. This state is most excellent, for the soul, being yet in the mortal body, tastes bliss with the immortals. Often it arrives at so great a union that it scarcely knows whether it is in the body or out of it. It tastes the pledge of eternal life, both because it is united with me, and because its will is dead in Christ. By that death its union is made with me, and indeed in no other way can it perfectly do so. Souls in this state of union taste life eternal. And they are divested of the hell of their own will, which gives to man the pledge of damnation if he yields to it."

How this devout servant of God seeks knowledge from God concerning the state and fruit of tears.

Then this servant of God, yearning with very great desire rose as if intoxicated both by the union which she had had with God, and by what she had heard and tasted of the supreme and sweet truth. And she yearned with grief over the ignorance of creatures in that they did not know their benefactor, or the affection of the love of God. Nevertheless she had joy from the hope of the promise that the Truth of God had made to her. For he had taught the way she was to direct her will (and the other servants of God as well as herself) so that he might show mercy to the world.

Lifting up the eye of her intellect upon the sweet Truth, to whom she remained united, this servant wished to know something of the states of the soul of which God had spoken to her. Seeing that the soul passes through these states with tears, she wished to learn from the Truth about the different kinds of tears. She desired to know how they came to be, and whence they proceeded, and the fruit that resulted from weeping. And she wished to know from the sweet, supreme and first Truth himself as to the manner of being of and reason for tears.

Inasmuch as the truth cannot be learned from any other than the Truth himself, and nothing can be learned in the Truth but what is seen by the eye of the intellect, she made her request of the Truth. For it is necessary for one who is lifted with desire to learn the truth with the light of faith. She had not forgotten the teaching that the Truth, that is, God, had given her, that in no other way could she learn about the different states and fruits of tears.

Therefore this servant rose out of herself, exceeding every limit of her nature with the greatness of her desire. And with the light of a lively faith, she opened the eye of her intellect upon the eternal Truth, in whom she saw and knew the truth, in the matter of her request. For God himself manifested it to her, and, condescending in his kindness to her burning desire, he fulfilled her petition.

How there are five kinds of tears.

Then said the supreme and sweet Truth of God, "Beloved and dearest daughter, you beg knowledge of the reasons and fruits of tears, and I have not despised your desire. Open wide the eye of your intellect and I will show you, the various kinds of tears.

"The first are the tears of the wicked of the world. These are the tears of damnation.

"The second are the imperfect tears caused by fear. These belong to those who abandon sin from fear of punishment and weep out of fear.

"The third are the tears of those who, having abandoned sin, are beginning to serve and taste me, and weep for very sweetness. But since their love is imperfect, so also is their weeping.

"The fourth are the tears of those who have arrived at the perfect love of their neighbor, loving me without any regard whatsoever for themselves. These weep and their weeping is perfect. The fifth are joined to the fourth and are tears of sweetness shed with great peace.

"I will explain all these to you. And I will tell you also of the tears of fire that involve no bodily tears of the eyes, but satisfy those who often would desire to weep and cannot.

"And I want you to know that all these various graces may exist in one soul, who, rising from fear and imperfect love, reaches perfect love in the union-producing state. Now I will begin to tell you about these tears."

Of the differences among these tears, arising from the explanation of the aforesaid state of the soul.

"I wish you to know that every tear proceeds from the heart, for there is no member of the body that will satisfy the heart so much as the eye. If the heart is in pain the eye manifests it. And if the pain is sensual the eye drops hearty tears that engender death. For, proceeding from the heart, they are caused by a disordinate love distinct from the love of me. Such love, being disordinate and an offense to me, receives the reward of mortal pain and tears. And these form that first class, who shed the tears of death.

"Now, begin to consider the tears that give the beginning of life, that is, the tears of those who, knowing their guilt, set to weeping for fear of the penalty they have incurred. These are both hearty and sensual tears, because the soul, not having yet arrived at perfect hatred of its guilt on account of the offense done to me, abandons its guilt with grief in its heart for the penalty that follows the sin committed. So the eye weeps in order to satisfy the grief of the heart.

"But the soul, exercising itself in virtue, begins to lose its fear, knowing that fear alone is not sufficient to give it eternal life. And so it proceeds, with love, to know itself and my goodness in it, and begins to take hope in my mercy, in which its heart feels joy. Sorrow for its grief, mingled with the joy of its hope in my mercy, causes its eye to weep. And these which tears issue from the very fountain of her heart.

"But, inasmuch as this soul has not yet arrived at great perfection, it often drops sensual tears. If you ask me why, I reply: Because the root of self-love is not sensual love, for that has already been removed. Rather, it is a spiritual love with which the soul desires spiritual consolations or loves some creature spiritually.

"Therefore, when such a soul is deprived of the thing it loves, that is, internal or external consolation (the internal being the consolation received from me, the external being that which it had from the creature), and when temptations and persecutions come on it, its heart is full of grief. And, as soon as its eye feels the grief and suffering of its heart, it begins to weep with a tender and compassionate sorrow, pitying itself with the spiritual compassion of self-love. For its self-will is not yet crushed and destroyed in everything, and in this way it sheds sensual tears— tears, that is, of spiritual passion.

"But, growing and exercising itself in the light of self-knowledge, the soul conceives displeasure at itself and finally perfect self-hatred. From this it draws true knowledge of my goodness with the fire of love. And then it begins to unite itself to me, and to conform its will to mine and so to feel joy and compassion. It feels joy in itself through the affection of love, and it feels compassion for its neighbor.

"Immediately its eye, wishing to satisfy the heart, cries with hearty love for me and for its neighbor, grieving solely for offenses done to me and for its neighbor's loss, and not for any penalty or loss due to itself. It no longer thinks of itself, but only of rendering glory and praise to my name.

"Then, in an ecstasy of desire, it joyfully takes the food prepared for it on the table of the holy cross. In so doing, it conforms itself to the humble, patient, and immaculate Lamb, my only-begotten

Son, of whom I made a bridge.

"Now this soul has traveled by that bridge, and has followed the doctrine of my Truth. It has endured with true and sweet patience every pain and trouble that I have permitted to be inflicted upon it for its salvation, manfully receiving them all. It has not chosen its afflictions according to its own tastes, but has accepted them according to mine. And not only has this soul endured its trials with patience, but has sustained them with joy. Therefore the soul counts it glory to be persecuted for my name's sake in whatever it may have to suffer.

"Then the soul arrives at such delight and tranquillity of mind that no tongue can describe it. The soul has crossed the river by means of the eternal Word, that is, by the doctrine of my only-begotten Son, and has fixed the eye of its intellect on me, the sweet supreme Truth. Having seen the Truth, the soul knows it; and knowing the Truth, the soul loves it. Drawing its affection after its intellect, it tastes my eternal deity, and it knows and sees the divine nature united to its humanity.

"Then the soul rests in me, the Sea of Peace, and its heart is united to me in love. When it in such a manner feels me, the eternal deity, its eyes shed tears of sweetness, tears indeed of milk, nourishing the soul in true patience. These tears are a sweet-smelling ointment, shedding odors of great sweetness.

"Oh, best beloved daughter, how glorious is the soul who has indeed been able to pass from the stormy ocean to me, the Sea of Peace, and in that sea, which is myself, the supreme and eternal deity, to fill the pitcher of its heart. And its eye, the conduit of its heart, endeavors to satisfy its heart-pangs, and so it sheds tears. This is the last stage in which the soul is both blessed and sorrowful.

"Blessed is the soul through the union that it feels itself to have with me, tasting the divine love. Sorrowful is the soul through the offenses that it sees done to my goodness and greatness, for in its self-knowledge it has seen and tasted the bitterness of such offenses. By this self-knowledge, together with its knowledge of me, it has arrived at the final stage.

"Yet sorrow is no impediment to the state of union that produces tears of great sweetness through self-knowledge, gained in love of one's neighbor. For in this exercise the soul discovers the plaint of my divine mercy, and grief at the offenses caused to its neighbor. And it weeps with those who weep, and rejoices with those who rejoice—that is, who live in my love. Over these the soul rejoices, seeing glory and praise rendered me by my servants.

"The third kind of grief does not prevent the fourth, that is, the final grief belonging to the unitive state. They give savor to each other, for, if this last grief (in which the soul finds such union with me), had not developed from the grief belonging to the third state of neighborly love, it would not be perfect. Therefore it is necessary that the one should flavor the other, or else the soul would come to a state of presumption, induced by the subtle breeze of love of its own reputation, and would fall at once, vomited from the heights to the depths. Therefore it is necessary to bear with others and to continually practice love of one's neighbor, together with true knowledge of oneself.

"In this way the soul will feel the fire of my love in itself, because love of its neighbor is developed out of love of me. That is, it is developed out of the learning that the soul obtained by knowing itself and my goodness in it. Therefore, when the soul sees itself inexpressibly loved by me, it loves every rational creature with the exact same love with which it sees itself loved.

"And, for this reason, the soul who knows me immediately expands to the love of its neighbor, because it sees that I love that neighbor indescribably. And so it loves still more the object that it sees me to have loved. It further knows that it can be of no use to me and can in no way repay me that pure love with which it feels herself to be loved by me. Therefore it endeavors to repay that love through the medium which I have given it, namely, its neighbor. For one's neighbor is the medium through which you can all serve me. You can perform all virtues by means of your neighbor. Therefore you should love your neighbor with the same pure love with which I have loved you. You cannot return that pure love directly to me, because I have loved you without being myself loved, and without any consideration of myself whatsoever.

"I loved you without being loved by you—
before you existed. It was, indeed, love that moved
me to create you in my own image and likeness. This
love you cannot repay to me, but you can pay it to
my rational creature. And this you can do by loving
your neighbor without being loved by him and
without consideration of your own advantage,
whether spiritual or temporal. You can love him
solely for the praise and glory of my name, because
he has been loved by me. In this way you will fulfill
the commandment of the law, to love me above
everything, and your neighbor as yourself.

"It is true indeed that this height cannot be
reached without passing through the second stage.
Nor can this height be preserved when it has been
reached if the soul abandons the affection from
which it has been developed, the affection to which
the second class of tears belongs. It is therefore
impossible to fulfill the law given by me, the eternal
God, without fulfilling the law of loving your neighbor. For these two laws were given you by my Truth,
Christ crucified. When united, these two states
nourish your soul in virtue, making it to grow in
the perfection of virtue and in the state of union.

"Not that the other state is changed because
this further state has been reached. No, this further
state only increases the riches of grace in new and
various gifts and admirable elevations of the mind.
It does so in the knowledge of the truth, which,
though it is mortal, appears immortal because the

soul's perception of its own sensuality is mortified, and its will is dead through the union that it has attained with me.

"Oh, how sweet is the taste of this union to the soul, for, in tasting it, it sees my secrets! Therefore it often receives the spirit of prophecy, knowing the things of the future. This is the effect of my goodness, but the humble soul should despise such things, not indeed in so far as they are given it by my love, but in so far as it desires them by reason of its appetite for consolation. It should consider itself unworthy of peace and quiet of mind, in order to nourish virtue within it.

"In such a case it must not remain in the second stage, but must return to the valley of self-knowledge. I give it this light, my grace permitting, so that it may ever grow in virtue. For the soul is never so perfect in this life that it cannot attain to a higher perfection of love.

"My only-begotten Son, your captain, was the only one who could not increase in perfection, because he was one with me, and I with him. Therefore his soul was blessed through union with the divine nature.

"But you, his pilgrim-members, must be ever ready to grow in greater perfection. This is not to say that you will move to another stage, for as I have said, you have now reached the last one. But you are to grow to that further grade of perfection in the last stage, which may please you by means of my grace."

*How the four stages of the soul, to which the
five states of tears belong, produce tears of
infinite value; and how God wishes to be served
as the Infinite, and not as anything finite.*

"These five states are like five principal canals filled with abundant tears of infinite value, all of which give life if they are disciplined in virtue. You ask how their value can be infinite. I do not say that in this life your tears can become infinite, but I call them infinite, on account of the infinite desire of your soul from which they proceed.

"I have already told you how tears come from the heart, and how the heart distributes them to the eye, having gathered them in its own fiery desire. When green wood is on the fire, the moisture it contains groans on account of the heat, because the wood is green. So does the heart, made green again by the renewal of grace drawn into the midst of its self-love. And grace dries up the soul, so that fiery desire and tears are united.

"Inasmuch as desire is never ended, it is never satisfied in this life. But the more the soul loves, the less it seems to itself to love. Thus is holy desire, which is founded in love, exercised, and with this desire the eye weeps. But when the soul is separated from the body and has reached me, its end, it does not on that account abandon desire, so as to no longer yearn for me or love its neighbor. For love has entered into it like a woman bearing the fruits of all other virtues.

"It is true that suffering is over and ended, for the soul who desires me possesses me in very truth, without any fear of ever losing what it has so long desired. But, in this way, hunger continues: Those who are hungry are satisfied, and as soon as they are satisfied, they hunger again. In this way their satisfaction is without disgust, and their hunger without suffering, for, in me, no perfection is lacking.

"Thus your desire is infinite, or otherwise it would be worth nothing. Nor would any virtue of yours have any life if you served me with anything finite. For I, who am the infinite God, wish to be served by you with infinite service. And the only infinite thing you possess is the affection and desire of your souls. In this sense there are tears of infinite value, and this is true because of the infinite desire that is united to the tears.

"When the soul leaves the body the tears remain behind, but the affection of love has drawn to itself the fruit of the tears, and has consumed it, just as happens to the water in your furnace: The water has not really been taken out of the furnace, but the heat of the fire has consumed it and drawn it into itself.

"Thus the soul, having arrived at tasting the fire of my divine charity, and having passed from this life in a state of love towards me and its neighbor, having further possessed that uniting love that caused its tears to fall, does not cease to offer me its blessed desires. It is tearful indeed, though without pain or physical weeping. For physical tears have evaporated in the furnace and have become tears of fire of the Holy Spirit.

"You see then how tears are infinite. For as regards the tears shed in this life only, no tongue can tell what different sorrows may cause them. I have now told you the difference among four of these states of tears."

Of the fruit of worldly men's tears.

"It remains for me to tell you of the fruit produced by tears shed with desire and received into the soul. But first will I speak to you of the first class of men whom I mentioned at the beginning of this discourse. I am referring to those who live miserably in the world, making a god of created things and of their own sensuality, from which comes damage to their body and soul. I said to you that every tear proceeds from the heart. And this is the truth, for the heart grieves in proportion to the love it feels. So worldly persons weep when their heart feels pain, that is, when they are deprived of something they love.

"But their complainings are many and diverse. Do you know how many? There are as many as there are different loves. And inasmuch as the root of self-love is corrupt, everything that grows from it is corrupt also. Self-love is a tree on which grows nothing but fruits of death, putrid flowers, stained leaves, and branches bowed down struck by various winds. This is the tree of the soul.

"For you are all trees of love, and without love you cannot live, for you have been made by me for love. The soul who lives virtuously places the root of its tree in the valley of true humility. But those who live miserably are planted on the mountain of pride.

"From this it follows that since the root of the tree is badly planted, the tree can bear no fruits of life, but only of death. Their fruits are their actions, which are all poisoned by many kinds of sin. And if they should produce some good fruit among their actions, even that good fruit will be spoiled by the foulness of its root. For no good action done by a soul in mortal sin is of value for eternal life, seeing that it is not done in grace.

"However, such a soul must not abandon its good works on this account. For every good deed is rewarded, and every evil deed is punished. A good action performed outside of a state of grace is not sufficient to merit eternal life. But my justice, my divine goodness, grants an incomplete reward, as imperfect as the action that obtains it. Often such a person is rewarded in temporal matters. Sometimes I give that soul more time in which to repent. And sometimes, I grant to that soul the life of grace by means of my servants who are pleasing and acceptable to me.

"I acted in this way with my glorious apostle Paul, who abandoned his refusal to believe, and the persecutions he directed against the Christians, upon hearing the prayer of St. Stephen. Therefore, in whatever state a person may be, he should never stop doing good.

"I said to you that the flowers of this tree are putrid, and so in truth they are. Its flowers are the stinking thoughts of the heart, displeasing to me and full of hatred and unkindness towards their neighbor. So if a person is a thief, he robs me of honor and takes it himself.

"This flower stinks less than that of false judgment, which is of two kinds. The first kind of false judgment is in regard to me. Those who are guilty of this false judgment judge my secret judgments and gauge falsely all my mysteries. That is, they judge that which I did in love, to have been done in hatred; that which I did in truth to have been done in falsehood; that which I give them for life, to have been given them for death. They condemn and judge everything according to their weak intellect; for they have blinded the eye of their intellect with sensual self-love, and hidden the pupil of the most holy faith, which they will not allow to see or know the truth.

"The second kind of false judgment is directed against one's neighbor. From this judgment often come many evils, because the wretched person wishes to set himself up as the judge of the affections and heart of other rational creatures, when he does not yet know himself. And, from an action that he may see, or from a word he may hear, he will judge the affection of the heart.

"My servants always judge well, because they are founded on me, the supreme good. But such as these always judge badly, for they are founded on evil. Such critics as these cause hatreds, murders, and unhappinesses of all kinds to their neighbors. And they remove themselves far away from the love of my servants' virtue.

"Truly these fruits follow the leaves, which are the words that issue from their mouth insulting me and the blood of my only-begotten Son, and showing hatred to their neighbors. And they think of nothing else but cursing and condemning my works, and blaspheming and saying evil of every rational creature, as their judgment may suggest to them.

"These unfortunate creatures do not remember that the tongue is made only to give honor to me, and to confess sins, and to be used in love of virtue, and for the salvation of one's neighbor. These are the stained leaves of that most miserable fault, because the heart from which they proceed is not clean, but all spotted with duplicity and misery.

"Apart from the spiritual privation of grace to the soul, how much danger of temporal loss may occur! For you have heard and seen how, through words alone, have come revolutions of states, destructions of cities, and many homicides and other evils. For a word entered the heart of the listener and passed through a space not large enough for a knife.

"This tree has seven branches drooping to the earth, on which grow the flowers and leaves. These branches are the seven mortal sins, which are full of many and diverse wickednesses. And these wickednesses are contained in the roots and trunk of self-love and of pride, which first made both branches and flowers of many thoughts, leaves of words, and fruits of wicked deeds.

"The seven branches stand drooping to the earth, because the branches of mortal sin can turn no other way than to the earth, the fragile, disordinate substance of the world. Do not marvel: they can turn no way but that in which they can be fed by the earth. For their hunger is insatiable, and the earth is unable to satisfy them.

"It is conformable to their state that they should always be unquiet, longing and desiring the thing with which they are filled to excess. This is why such excess cannot content them. For they (who are infinite in their being) are always desiring something finite. Yet their being will never end, though their life to grace ends when they commit mortal sin.

"Man is placed above all creatures, and not beneath them, and he cannot be satisfied or content except in something greater than himself. Greater than himself there is nothing but myself, the eternal

God. Therefore I alone can satisfy him. And, because he is deprived of this satisfaction by his guilt, he remains in continual torment and pain. Weeping follows pain, and when he begins to weep the wind strikes the tree of self-love, which he has made the principle of all his being."

How this devout servant of God, thanking God for his explanation of the above-mentioned states of tears, makes three petitions.

Then this servant of God, eager with the greatness of her desire, through the sweetness of the explanation and satisfaction that she had received from the Truth, concerning the state of tears, said as one full of love—"Thanks, thanks be to you, supreme and eternal Father, satisfier of holy desires, and lover of our salvation, who, through your love, gave us Love himself. And you did this in the time of our warfare with you, in the person of your only-begotten Son.

"By this abyss of your fiery love, I beg of you grace and mercy to come to you truly in the light, and not to flee far in darkness away from your doctrine. You have clearly demonstrated to me the truth of your doctrine, so that, by its light, I may perceive two other points. Concerning these, I fear that they are, or may become, stumbling-blocks to me.

"I beg, eternal Father, that, before I leave the subject of these states of tears, you would explain these points also to me. The first is—when a person who desires to serve you comes to me or to some other servant of yours to ask for counsel, how should I teach him?

"I know, sweet and eternal God, that you replied earlier to this question—'I am the One who takes delight in few words and many deeds.' Nevertheless, if it may please your goodness to grant me a few more words on the subject, it will cause me the greatest pleasure.

"And also, on some occasion when I am praying for your creatures, and in particular for your servants, and I seem to see the subjects of my prayer, in one I may find (in the course of my prayer) a well-disposed mind, a soul rejoicing in you. And in another, I may find, as it might seem to me, a mind full of darkness. Do I have the right, eternal Father, to judge one soul to be in light, and the other in darkness?

"Or, supposing I should see that the one lives in great penance, and the other does not. Would I be right to judge that the one does the greater penance has the higher perfection? I pray you, so that I may not be deceived through my limited vision, that you would declare to me in detail what you have already said in general on this matter.

"The second request I have to make is that you will explain further to me about the sign that you said the soul receives on being visited by you—the sign that reveals your presence. If I remember well, eternal Truth, you said that the soul remains in joy and courageous virtue. I would gladly know whether this joy can consist with the delusion of the passion of spiritual self-love. If it were so, I would humbly confine myself to the sign of virtue.

"These are the things that I beg you to tell me, so that I may serve you and my neighbor in truth, and not fall into false judgment concerning your creatures and servants. It seems to me that the habit of judging keeps the soul far from you, so I do not wish to fall into this snare."

How the light of reason is necessary to every
soul who wishes to serve God in truth; and first
of the light of reason in general.

Then the eternal God, delighting in the thirst and hunger of that servant, and in the purity of her heart, and in the desire with which she longed to serve him, turned the eye of his kindness and mercy upon her, and said—"Best-beloved, dearest and sweetest daughter, my spouse! Rise out of yourself and open the eye of your intellect to see me, the infinite goodness, and the inexpressible love that I have towards you and my other servants. And open the ear of the desire that you feel towards me, and remember that if you do not see, you cannot hear.

That is, the soul who does not see into my truth with the eye of its intellect, cannot hear or know my Truth. Therefore, so that you may know it better, rise above the feelings of your senses.

"And I, who take delight in your request, will satisfy your demand. Not that you can increase my delight—for I am the cause of you and of your increase of delight, not you of mine. Yet the very pleasure that I take in the work of my own hands causes me delight."

Then that soul obeyed and rose out of herself, in order to learn the true solution of her difficulty. And the eternal God said to her, "So that you may understand better what I shall say to you, I shall revert to the beginning of your request concerning the three lights that issue from me, the true Light. The first is a general light dwelling in those who live in ordinary charity. The other two lights dwell in those who, having abandoned the world, desire perfection.

"You know that without the light, no one can walk in the truth—that is, without the light of reason. And that light you draw from me, the true light, by means of the eye of your intellect and the light of faith that I have given you in holy baptism—though you may have lost it by your own defects. For, in baptism, and through the mediation of the blood of my only-begotten Son, you have received the form of faith. You exercise faith in virtue by the light of reason, which gives you life and causes you to walk in the path of truth. By its mean you arrive at me, the true light. Without it, you would plunge into darkness.

"It is necessary for you to have two lights derived from this primary light, and to these two I will also add a third. The first lightens you to know the transitory nature of the things of the world, all of which pass like the wind. But this you cannot know thoroughly, unless you first recognize your own fragility. You must know how strong is your inclination, through the law of perversity with which your members are bound, to rebel against me, your creator. (Not that by this law anyone can be constrained to commit even the smallest sin against his will—but this law of perversity fights lustily against the spirit.)

"I did not impose this law upon you so that my rational creature should be conquered by it, but so he should prove and increase the virtue of his soul. For virtue cannot be proved, except by its opposite.

"Sensuality is contrary to the spirit, and yet, by means of sensuality, the soul is able to prove the love that it has for me, its creator. How does it prove it? When, with anger and displeasure, it rises against itself. This law has also been imposed in order to preserve the soul in true humility.

"Therefore you see that, while I created the soul in my own image and likeness, placing it in such dignity and beauty, I caused it to be accompanied by the vilest of all things, imposing on it the law of perversity. I imprisoned it in a body, formed of the vilest substance of the earth, so that, seeing in what its true beauty consisted, it should not raise her head in pride against me. Wherefore, to one who possesses this light, the fragility of his body is a cause of humiliation to the soul, and is in no way matter for pride, but rather for true and perfect humility. So this law does not constrain you to any sin by its strivings, but supplies a reason to make you know yourselves and the instability of the world.

"This should be seen by the eye of the intellect, with the light of holy faith, which is the pupil of the eye. This is the light that is necessary to every rational creature, whatever may be his condition, who wishes to participate in the life of grace, in the fruit of the blood of the immaculate Lamb.

"This is the ordinary light, that is, the light that all persons must possess. For, without it, the soul would be in a state of damnation. This is because the soul, being without the light, is not in a state of grace. For, not having the light, it knows neither the evil of its sin nor the cause of its sin, and therefore cannot avoid or hate it.

"And similarly, if the soul does not know good and the reason for good, that is to say virtue, it cannot love or desire me, who am the essential good. Nor can it love or desire virtue, which I have given you as an instrument and means for you to receive both my grace and myself, the true good.

"See then how necessary is this light, for your sins consist in nothing else than in loving what I hate, and in hating what I love. I love virtue and hate vice. One who loves vice and hates virtue offends me and is deprived of my grace. Such a one walks as if blind, for he does not know the cause of vice, that is, his sensual self-love, nor does he hate himself on account of it. He is ignorant of vice and of the evil which follows it. He is ignorant of virtue and of me, who am the cause of his obtaining life-giving virtue. And he is ignorant of his own dignity, which he should maintain by advancing to grace, by means of virtue. See, therefore, how his ignorance is the cause of all his evil, and how you also need this light."

Of those who have placed their desire in the mortifi-cation of the body rather than in the destruction of their own will; and of the second light, which is more perfect than the general one.

"When the soul has arrived at the attainment of the general light of which I have spoken, it should not remain contented. For as long as you are pilgrims in this life, you are capable of growth. One who does not go forward, by that very fact, is turning back. The soul should either grow in the general light, which it has acquired through my grace, or strive anxiously to attain to the second and perfect light. For, if the soul truly has light, it will wish to arrive at perfection.

"In this second, perfect light are to be found two kinds of perfection. One perfection is that of those who give themselves up wholly to the castigation of the body, doing great and severe penance. These, so that their sensuality may not rebel against their reason, have placed their desire in the mortification of the body rather than in the destruction of their self-will. They feed their souls at the table of penance, and are good and perfect. And this is true provided that they act with true knowledge of themselves and of me, with great humility, and wholly conformed to the judgment of my will, and not to that of the will of man.

"But, if such souls were not clothed with my will, in true humility, they would often offend against their own perfection, esteeming themselves the judges of those who do not walk in the same path. Do you know why this would happen to them? Because they have placed all their labor and desire in the mortification of the body, rather than in the destruction of their own will. Such as these wish always to choose their own times, and places, and consolations, after their own fashion, and also the persecutions of the world and of the devil.

"They say, cheating themselves with the delusion of their own self-will, which I have already called their spiritual self-will, 'I wish to have that consolation, and not these battles, or these temptations of the devil. Not, indeed, for my own pleasure, but in order to please God the more, and in order to retain him the more in my soul through grace. For it seems to me that I should possess him more, and serve him better in that way than in this.'

"And this is the way the soul often falls into trouble, and becomes tedious and intolerable to itself; thus injuring its own perfection. Yet it does not perceive that, within it lurks the stench of pride, and there it lies.

"Now, if the soul were not in this condition, but were truly humble and not presumptuous, it would be illuminated to see that I, the primary and sweet Truth, grant condition, and time, and place, and consolations, and tribulations as they may be needed for your salvation, and to complete the perfection to which I have elected the soul. And it would see that I give everything through love, and that therefore it should receive everything with love and reverence.

"This is what the souls in the second state do, and, by doing so, they arrive at the third state. I will now speak to you of these souls, explaining to you the nature of these two states which stand in the most perfect light."

Of the third and most perfect state, and of reason, and of the works done by the soul who has arrived at this light. And of a beautiful vision which this devout servant of God once received, in which the method of arriving at perfect purity is fully treated. And of the means to avoid judging our neighbor.

"Those who belong to the third state, which immediately follows the last, having arrived at this glorious light, are perfect in every condition in which they may be. They receive every event that I permit to happen to them with due reverence. These deem themselves worthy of the troubles and stumbling-blocks that the world causes them, and of the privation of their own consolation, and indeed of whatever circumstance happens to them.

"And inasmuch as these souls deem themselves worthy of trouble, so also do they deem themselves unworthy of the fruit that they receive after their trouble. They have known and tasted in the light my eternal will, which desires nothing but your good. It gives and permits these troubles in order that you should be sanctified in me.

"Therefore the soul, having known my will, clothes itself with it. It fixes its attention on nothing else except seeing in what way it can preserve and increase its perfection to the glory and praise of my name. It opens the eye of its intellect and fixes it in the light of faith upon Christ crucified, my only-begotten Son. It loves and follows his doctrine, which is the rule for the perfect and the imperfect alike.

"Then my Truth, the Lamb, who became enamored of this soul when he saw it, gives it the doctrine of perfection. The soul knows what this perfection is, having seen it practiced by the sweet and amorous Word, my only-begotten Son.

"For he was fed at the table of holy desire and sought the honor of me, the eternal Father, and your salvation. Inflamed with this desire, he ran, with great eagerness, to the shameful death of the cross, and accomplished the obedience imposed on him by me, his Father. He shunned neither labors nor insults, nor withdrew on account of your ingratitude or ignorance of so great a benefit. Neither did he withdraw because of the persecutions of the Jews, or on account of the insults, derision, grumbling, and shouting of the people.

"But all this he passed through like the true captain and knight that he was. For I placed him on the battle-field to deliver you from the hands of the devil, so that you might be freed from the most terrible slavery in which you could ever be. And I gave him to you to teach you his road, his doctrine, and his rule, so that you might open the door of me, eternal Life, with the key of his precious blood, shed with such fire of love, with such hatred of your sins.

"It was as if the sweet and loving Word, my Son, had said to you: 'Behold, I have made the road, and opened the door with my blood.' Do not then be negligent to follow. Do not lay down to rest in self-love and ignorance of the road, presuming to choose to serve me in your own way, instead of in the way that I have made straight for you by means of my Truth, the incarnate Word, and built up with his blood. Rise up then, promptly, and follow him, for no one can reach me, the Father, if not by him. He is the way and the door by which you must enter into me, the Sea of Peace.

"When therefore the soul has arrived at seeing, knowing, and tasting this light in its full sweetness, it runs, as one inflamed with love, to the table of holy desire. Like one who has placed his all in this light and knowledge and has destroyed his own will, it shuns no labor, from whatever source it comes. It endures the troubles, the insults, the temptations of the devil, and the murmurings of men. It eats at the table of the most holy cross, the food of the honor of me, the eternal God, and of the salvation of souls.

"It seeks no reward, either from me or from creatures, because it is stripped of mercenary love, that is, of love for me based on self-interested motives. It is clothed in perfect light and loves me in perfect purity, with no other regard than for the praise and glory of my name. It serves neither me for its own delight, nor its neighbor for its own profit, but purely through love alone.

"Such as these have lost themselves, and have stripped themselves of the Old Man, that is, of their own sensuality. Having clothed themselves with the New Man, sweet Christ Jesus, my Truth, they follow him manfully.

"These sit at the table of holy desire, having been more anxious to slay their own will than to slay and mortify their own body. They have indeed mortified their body, though not as an end in itself, but as a means to help them keep their own will at bay. Their principal desires should be to slay their own will, so that it may not seek or wish anything else than to follow my sweet Truth, Christ crucified, and to seek the honor and glory of my name and the salvation of souls.

"Those who are in this sweet light know it, and remain constantly in peace and quiet. No one scandalizes them, for they have cut away the thing by which stumbling-blocks are caused, namely their own will. And all the persecutions with which the world and the devil can attack them, slide under their feet and do not hurt them. For they remain attached to me by the umbilical cord of fiery desire.

"Such a one rejoices in everything, and does not make himself judge of my servants or of any rational creature. Rather, he rejoices in every condition and in every manner of holiness that he sees, saying: 'Thanks be to you, eternal Father, who have in your house many mansions.'

"And he rejoices more in the different ways of holiness that he sees, than if he were to see everyone traveling by one road. He finds, in this way, that he perceives the greatness of my goodness become more manifest. Thus, rejoicing, he draws from all the fragrance of the rose.

"And not only in the case of good, but even when he sees something evidently sinful he does not fall into judgment. Rather, he shows true and holy compassion and intercedes with me for sinners. And he says, with perfect humility: 'Today it is your turn, and tomorrow it will be mine, unless divine grace preserves me.'

"Dearest daughter, love this sweet and excellent state. Gaze at those who run in this glorious light and holiness, for they have holy minds, and eat at the table of holy desire. They have arrived at feeding on the food of souls, which the honor of me, the eternal Father. And they are clothed with burning love in the sweet garment of my Lamb, my only-begotten Son, namely his doctrine. These do not lose their time in passing false judgments, either on my servants or the servants of the world. And they are never scandalized by any murmurings of men, either for their own sake or that of others.

"And since their love is so ordered, these souls, my dearest daughter, never take offense at those they love, nor at any rational creature, for their will is dead and not alive. They never assume the right to judge the will of men, but only the will of my clemency.

"These souls observe the doctrine that was given you by my Truth at the beginning of your life, when you were thinking in what way you could arrive at perfect purity, and were praying to me with a great desire of doing so. You know what I replied to you, while you were asleep, concerning this holy desire. And you know that the words resounded not only in your mind, but also in your ear. So much so, that you returned to your waking body.

"And my Truth said, 'Will you arrive at perfect purity, and be freed from stumbling-blocks, so that your mind may not be scandalized by anything? Unite yourself always to me by the affection of love, for I am supreme and eternal purity. I am the fire that purifies the soul. The closer the soul is to me, the purer it becomes. And the farther it is from me, the more its purity leaves it.'

"The reason persons of the world fall into such iniquities is that they are separated from me. But the soul who, without any medium, unites itself directly to me, participates in my purity.

"Another thing is necessary for you to arrive at this union and purity, namely, you should never judge the will of man in anything that you may see done or said by any creature whatsoever, either to yourself or to others. You should consider my will alone, both in them and in yourself. And if you should see evidence of sins or defects, draw the rose out of those thorns. That is, offer them to me, with holy compassion.

"In the case of injuries done to you, judge that my will permits them in order to prove virtue in you, and in my other servants. Esteem that one who acts in an injurious manner does so as the instrument of my will. Such apparent sinners may frequently have good intentions, for no one can judge the secrets of the heart of man. What you do not see you should not judge in your mind, even though externally it may be open, mortal sin.

"See nothing in others but my will, not in order to judge, but with holy compassion. In this way you will arrive at perfect purity. For, acting in this way your mind will not be scandalized, either by me or by your neighbor. Otherwise you fall into contempt of your neighbor, if you judge his evil will towards you, instead of acknowledging my will acting in him.

"Such contempt and scandal separates the soul from me and prevents perfection. And, in some cases, it deprives a person of grace, more or less according to the gravity of his contempt and the hatred that his judgment has conceived against his neighbor.

"A different reward is received by the soul who perceives only my will, which wishes nothing else but your good. Everything I give or permit to happen to you, I give so that you may arrive at the end for which I created you. And because the soul remains always in the love of its neighbor, it remains always in mine, and thus it remains united to me.

"Therefore, in order to arrive at purity, you must entreat me to do three things: First, to grant you to be united to me by the affection of love, retaining in your memory the benefits you have received from me. Second, with the eye of your intellect to see the affection of my love, with which I love you inestimably. And third, in the will of others to discern my will only, and not their evil will. For I am their judge, not you. And in doing this, you will arrive at all perfection.

"This was the doctrine given to you by my Truth. Now I tell you, dearest daughter, that those who have learned this doctrine, taste the pledge of eternal life in this life. And, if you have retained this doctrine well, you will not fall into the snares of the devil, because you will recognize them in the case about which you have asked me.

"But nevertheless, in order to satisfy your desire more clearly, I will tell you and show you how men should never discern by judgment, but with holy compassion."

In what way those who stand in the third and most perfect light, receive the pledge of eternal life while in this life.

"Why did I say to you that they received the pledge of eternal life? I say that they receive the pledge, but not the full payment, because they wait to receive it in me, who am eternal Life. In me they have life without death, and are filled, but not to excess. In me they have hunger without pain, for from that divine hunger pain is far away. Though they have what they desire, their fulfillment contains no excess, for I am the flawless food of life.

"It is true that in this life they receive the pledge and taste it in that the soul begins to hunger for the honor of the eternal God and for the food of the salvation of other souls. And being hungry, it eats. That is, it nourishes itself with love of its neighbor, which causes its hunger and desire. For the love of one's neighbor is a food that never fills to excess the one who feeds on it. Thus the eater cannot be completely filled, and always remains hungry.

"So this pledge is the commencement of a guarantee that is given to mankind. In virtue of this pledge he expects one day to receive his payment. His expectation is not based on the perfection of the pledge in itself, but on faith, on the certainty that which he has of reaching the completion of his being and receiving his payment.

"Therefore this loving soul, clothed in my truth, has already received in this life the pledge of my love and of its neighbor's. This soul is not yet perfect, but awaits perfection in immortal life.

"I say that this pledge is not perfect, because the soul who tastes it does not yet have, the perfection that would prevent its feeling pain in itself, or in others: In itself, through the offense done to me by the law of perversity that is bound in its members and struggles against the spirit; and in others by the offense of its neighbor.

"The soul has indeed, in a sense, perfect grace. But it does not have the perfection of my saints, those who have arrived at me, who am eternal Life. For their desires are without suffering, and yours are not. These servants of mine, who nourish themselves at this table of holy desire, are both blessed and full of grief, even as my only-begotten Son was on the wood of the holy cross. There, while his flesh was in grief and torment, his soul was blessed through its union with the divine nature.

"In like manner these servants are blessed by the union of their holy desire towards me. They are clothed, in my sweet will. And they are full of grief through compassion for their neighbor, and because they afflict their own self-love, depriving it of sensual delights and consolations."

How this servant of God, rendering thanks to
God, humbles herself; then she prays for the whole
world and particularly for the mystical body of
the holy church, for her spiritual children,
and for the two fathers of her soul; and, after
these things, she asks to hear something about the
defects of the ministers of the holy church.

Then that servant of God, as if actually intoxicated, seemed beside herself. It was as if the feelings of her body were alienated through the union of love that she had made with her creator. And it was as if, in elevating her mind, she had gazed into the eternal truth with the eye of her intellect, and, having recognized the truth, had become deeply in love with it.

And she said, "Supreme one! You, supreme and eternal Father, have manifested to me your truth, the hidden deceits of the devil, and the deceitfulness of personal feeling. You have done this so that I, and others in this life of pilgrimage, may know how to avoid being deceived by the devil or ourselves! What moved you to do so? Love, because you loved me without my having loved you.

"Fire of love! Thanks, thanks be to you, eternal Father! I am imperfect and full of darkness, and you, perfection and light, have shown to me perfection, and the resplendent way of the doctrine of your only-begotten Son.

"I was dead, and you have brought me to life. I was sick, and you have given me medicine. And yours was not only the medicine of the Blood that you gave for the diseased human race in the person of your Son, but also a medicine against a secret infirmity of which I was unaware.

"For you have shown me that, in no way, can I judge any rational creature, and particularly your servants, upon whom I often passed judgment under the pretext of your honor and the salvation of souls. Therefore, I thank you, supreme and eternal good, that, in manifesting your truth, the deceitfulness of the devil, and our own passions, you have made me know my infirmity.

"Therefore I beseech you through grace and mercy that, from today forward, I may never again wander from the path of your doctrine, which was given by your goodness to me and to whoever wishes to follow it. And I beseech you to grant this because without you is nothing is done. To you, then, eternal Father, I have recourse and flee.

"I do not beseech you for myself alone, Father, but for the whole world, and particularly for the mystical body of the holy church, that this truth given to me, miserable one that I am, by you, eternal truth, may shine in your ministers.

"Also I beseech you especially for all those whom you have given me, and whom you have made one with me, and whom I love with a particular love. For they will be my refreshment to the glory and praise of your name, when I see them running on this sweet and straight road, pure, and dead to their own will and opinion, and without any passing judgment on their neighbor or causing him any scandal or murmuring. And I pray you, sweetest love, that not one of them may be taken from me by the hand of the infernal devil, so that at last they may arrive at you, their end, eternal Father.

"I now know for certain, eternal Truth, that you will not despise the desire of the petitions that I have made to you, because I know, from seeing what it has pleased you to manifest, and still more from proof, that you are the acceptor of holy desires. I, your unworthy servant, will strive, according as you will give me grace, to observe your commandments and your doctrine.

"Now, eternal Father, I remember a word that you said to me in speaking of the ministers of the holy church, to the effect that you would speak to me more distinctly, in some other place, of the sins that they commit today. If it should please your goodness to tell me anything of this matter, I will gladly hear it, so as to have material for increasing my grief, compassion, and anxious desire for their salvation. I remember that you said that, on account of the endurance, the tears, the grief, the sweat and the prayers of your servants, you would reform the holy church, and comfort her with good and holy pastors. I ask you this so that these sentiments may increase in me."

How God renders this servant attentive to prayer,
replying to one of the above-mentioned petitions.

Then the eternal God turned the eye of his mercy
upon this servant. Not despising her desire, but
granting her requests, he proceeded to satisfy the last
petition that she had made concerning his promise,
saying: "Best beloved and dearest daughter, I will
fulfill your desire in this request, so that, on your
side, you may not sin through ignorance or negligence. For a fault of yours would be more serious
and worthy of graver reproof now than before,
because you have learned more of my truth.

"Apply yourself attentively to pray for all
rational creatures, for the mystical body of the holy
church, and for those friends whom I have given
you, whom you love with particular love. And be
careful not to be negligent in giving them the benefit of your prayers, the example of your life, and the
teaching of your words, reproving vice and encour-
aging virtue according to your power.

"Concerning the supports that I have given you,
of whom you spoke to me, know that you are truly
a means by which they may each receive, according
to their needs and fitness. And I, your creator, grant
you this opportunity, for without me you can do
nothing. I will fulfill your desires, but do not fail, or
they either, in your hope in me. And my providence
will never fail you.

"So every person, if he is humble, shall receive what he is fit to receive. And every minister shall receive what I have given him to administer, each in his own way, according to what he has received and will receive from my goodness."

How this devout servant, praising and thanking God, made a prayer for the holy church.

Then this servant, as if intoxicated, tormented, and on fire with love, her heart wounded with great bitterness, turned to the supreme and eternal Goodness, and said: "Eternal God! Light above every other light! Fire above every fire! You are the only fire that burns without consuming, and consumes all sin and self-love found in the soul. You do not afflict the soul, but you fatten it with insatiable love. And though the soul is filled it is not sated. The more of you it has, the more it seeks. And the more it desires, the more it finds and tastes of you, supreme and eternal fire, abyss of charity.

"Supreme and eternal good, who has moved you, infinite God, to illuminate me, your finite creature, with the light of your truth? You, the same fire of love, are the cause. For it is love that has always constrained and continues to constrain you to create us in your image and likeness, and to show us mercy by giving immeasurable and infinite graces to your rational creatures.

"Goodness above all goodness! You alone are supremely good, and nevertheless you gave the Word, your only-begotten Son, to associate with us filthy ones who are filled with darkness. What was the cause of this? Love. Because you loved us before we were.

"Eternal greatness! You made yourself low and small to make mankind great. On whichever side I turn I find nothing but the abyss and fire of your love. And can a wretch like me pay back to you the graces and the burning love that you have shown and continue to show in particular to me, and the love that you show to all your creatures? No, but you alone, most sweet and loving Father, will be thankful and grateful for me that is, that the affection of your charity itself will render you thanks. My being, and every further grace that you have bestowed upon me, I have from you. And you give them to me through love, and not as my due.

"Sweetest Father, when the human race lay sick through the sin of Adam, you sent it a physician, the sweet and loving Word—your Son. And when I was lying infirm with the sickness of negligence and much ignorance, you, most soothing and sweet physician, eternal God, gave a soothing, sweet, and bitter medicine, that I may be cured and rise from my infirmity. You soothed me because with your love and gentleness you manifested yourself to me, sweet above all sweetness. You illuminated the eye of my intellect with the light of most holy faith.

"As it has pleased you to manifest your light to me, I have known the excellence of grace that you have given to the human race. For you administer to it the entire God-Man in the mystical body of the holy church. And I have known the dignity of your ministers, whom you have appointed to administer you to us. I desired that you would fulfill the promise that you made to me, and you gave much more, more even than I knew how to ask for.

"Therefore I know in truth that the human heart does not know how to ask or desire as much as you can give. And thus I see that you are the supreme and eternal good, and that we are not. And because you are infinite, and we are finite, you give what your rational creatures cannot desire enough, filling us with things for which we do not ask you.

"Moreover, I have received light from your greatness and charity, through the love that you have for the whole human race, and in particular for your anointed ones, who ought to be earthly angels in this life. You have shown me the virtue and the blessed state of these your anointed ones, who have lived like burning lamps, shining with the pearl of justice in the holy church.

"And by comparison with these I have better understood the sins of those who live wretchedly. Therefore I have conceived a very great sorrow at offenses done to you, and at the harm done to the whole world. And because you have manifested and grieved over their iniquities—to me, a wretch who am the cause and instrument of many sins—I am plunged into intolerable grief.

"You, inestimable love, have manifested this to me, giving me a sweet and bitter medicine. You have done this so that I might wholly arise out of the infirmity of my ignorance and negligence, knowing myself and your goodness and the offenses that are committed against you. And you have desired that I might shed a river of tears over my wretched self and over those who are dead, in that they live miserably.

"Therefore I do not wish, eternal Father, inexpressible fire of love, that my heart should ever grow weary, or my eyes fail through tears, in desiring your honor and the salvation of souls. But I beg of you, by your grace, that these may be as two streams of water issuing from you, the Sea of Peace.

"Thanks, thanks to you, Father, for granting me what I asked you and what I neither knew nor asked. For by thus giving me matter for grief you have invited me to offer before you sweet, loving, and yearning desires, with humble and continual prayer. Now I beg of you to show mercy to the world and to the holy church. I pray you to fulfill what you caused me to ask you.

"Alas! what a wretched and sorrowful soul is mine, the cause of all these evils. Do not put off any longer your merciful designs towards the world, but descend and fulfill the desire of your servants.

"I know well that mercy is your own attribute, and thus you can not destroy it or refuse it to one who asks for it. Your servants knock at the door of your truth, because in the truth of your only-begotten Son they know the inexpressible love that you have for mankind. As a result, the fire of your love ought not and cannot refrain from opening to one who knocks with perseverance.

"Therefore open, unlock, and break the hardened hearts of your creatures, not for their sakes who do not knock, but on account of your infinite goodness. Grant the prayer of those, eternal Father who, as you see, stand at the door of your truth and pray. For what do they pray? For with the blood of this door—your Truth—you have washed our iniquities and destroyed the stain of Adam's sin. The blood is ours, for you have made it our bath, and thus you can not deny it to any one who truly asks for it.

"Give, then, the fruit of your blood to your creatures. Place in the balance the price of the blood of your Son, so that the infernal devils may not carry off your lambs. You are the good shepherd who, to fulfill your obedience, laid down his life for your lambs, and made for us a bath of his blood.

"That blood is what your hungry servants beg of you at this door. They beg you through it to show mercy to the world, and to cause your holy church to bloom with the fragrant flowers of good and holy pastors, who by their sweet odor shall extinguish the stench of the putrid flowers of sin.

"You have said, eternal Father, that through the love that you have for your rational creatures, and the prayers and the many virtues and labors of your servants, you would show mercy to the world and reform the church, and thus give us refreshment. Therefore do not delay, but turn the eye of your mercy towards us, for you must first reply to us before we can cry out with the voice of your mercy.

"Open the door of your inestimable love which you have given us through the door of your Word. I know indeed that you open before we can even knock. For it is with the affection of love that you have given to your servants, that they knock and cry to you, seeking your honor and the salvation of souls.

"Give them then the bread of life, that is to say, the fruit of the blood of your only-begotten Son, which they ask of you for the praise and glory of your name and the salvation of souls. For more glory and praise will be yours in saving so many creatures, than in leaving them obstinate in their hardness of heart.

"To you, eternal Father, everything is possible, and even though you have created us without our own help, you will not save us without it. I beg of you to force their wills, and dispose them to wish for that for which they do not wish. And this I ask you through your infinite mercy.

"You have created us from nothing. Now, therefore, that we are in existence, show mercy to us, and remake the vessels which you have created in your image and likeness. Re-create them to grace in your mercy and in the blood of your Son, sweet Christ Jesus."

A TREATISE OF
OBEDIENCE

*Here begins the treatise of obedience, and first
of where obedience may be found, and what
it is that destroys it, and what is the sign
of one's possessing it, and what
accompanies and nourishes obedience*

The supreme and eternal Father, kindly turning
the eye of his mercy and clemency towards his
servant, replied: "Your holy desire and righteous
request, dearest daughter, have a right to be heard.
And inasmuch as I am the supreme Truth, I will keep
my word, fulfilling the promise that I made to you
and satisfying your desire. And if you ask me where
obedience is to be found, and what is the cause of its
loss, and the sign of its possession, I reply that you
will find it in its completeness in the sweet and loving
Word, my only-begotten Son. So prompt in him was
this virtue, that, in order to fulfill it, he hastened to
the shameful death of the cross.

"What destroys obedience? Look at the first man and you will see the cause that destroyed the obedience imposed on him by me, the eternal Father. It was pride, which was produced by self-love, and desire to please his companion. This was the cause that deprived him of the perfection of obedience, giving him instead disobedience, depriving him of the life of grace, and slaying his innocence. As a consequence, he fell into impurity and great misery, and not only he, but the whole human race.

"The sign that you have the virtue of obedience is patience, and impatience is the sign that you do not have it. No one at all can reach eternal life if he does not have the virtue of obedience. For the door to eternal life was unlocked by the key of obedience, which had been fastened by the disobedience of Adam. Then, being constrained by my infinite goodness, since I saw that mankind, whom I so much loved, did not return to me, his end, I took the keys of obedience and placed them in the hands of my sweet and loving Word—the Truth. And becoming the porter of that door, he opened it.

"No one can enter into eternal life except by means of that door and that porter. That is why he said in the holy Gospel that no one could come to the Father, if not by him. When he returned to me, rising to heaven from among mankind at the Ascension, he left you this sweet key of obedience.

"Now I wish you to see and know this most excellent virtue in that humble and immaculate

Lamb, and the source from which it proceeds. What caused the great obedience of the Word? The love that he had for my honor and for your salvation. Whence proceeded this love? From the clear vision with which his soul saw the divine essence and the eternal Trinity, thus always looking on me, the eternal God.

"His faithfulness obtained this vision most perfectly for him, which vision you imperfectly enjoy by the light of holy faith. He was faithful to me, his eternal Father, and therefore hastened as one in love along the road of obedience, lit up with the light of glory.

"And inasmuch as love cannot be alone, but is accompanied by all the true and royal virtues—because all the virtues draw their life from love—he possessed them all, but in a different way from that in which you do. Among the other virtues he possessed patience, which is the marrow of obedience, and a sign, that shows whether a soul is in a state of grace and truly loves or not.

"Consequently, charity, the mother of patience, has given patience as a sister to obedience, and has so closely united them together that one cannot be lost without the other. Either you have them both or you have neither.

"The virtue of obedience has a nurse who feeds it, that is, true humility. Therefore a soul is obedient in proportion to its humility, and humble in proportion to its obedience.

"Humility is the foster-mother and nurse of charity, and with the same milk it feeds the virtue of obedience. The garments given it by this nurse are self-contempt and insult and the desire to displease itself, and to please me.

"Where does it find these attributes? In sweet Christ Jesus, my only-begotten Son. For who abased himself more than he did? He was heaped with insults, jibes, and mockings. He caused pain to himself in his bodily life, in order to please me. And who was more patient than he? for his cry was never heard in murmuring. Rather, he patiently embraced his injuries like one filled with love, fulfilling the obedience imposed on him by me, his eternal Father. As a result, in him you will find obedience perfectly accomplished.

"He left you this rule and this doctrine—which gives you life, for it is the straight way—having first observed them himself. He is the way, and therefore he said, 'I am the way, the truth, and the life.' For one who travels by that way, travels in the light. And being enlightened, he cannot stumble or be caused to fall, without perceiving it. For he has cast from himself the darkness of self-love, by which he fell into disobedience.

"Just as I spoke to you of a companion virtue proceeding from obedience and humility, so I now tell you that disobedience comes from pride, which issues from self-love and deprives the soul of humility. The sister given by self-love to disobedience is impatience, and pride, its foster-mother, feeds it with the darkness of unfaithfulness. So it hastens along the way of darkness, which leads it to eternal death. All this you should read in that glorious book, where you find described this and every other virtue."

How obedience is the key with which heaven is opened, and how the soul should fasten it by means of a cord to its waist, and of the excellences of obedience.

"Now that I have shown you where obedience is to be found, whence it comes, who is its companion, and who is its foster-mother, I will continue to speak of the obedient and of the disobedient together. And I will speak of obedience in general, which is the obedience of the precepts, and in particular, which is that of the counsels. The whole of your faith is founded upon obedience, for by it you prove your faithfulness.

"You are all by my truth to obey the commandments of the law, the chief of which is to love me above everything, and your neighbor as yourself. And the commandments are so bound up together that you cannot observe or transgress one without observing or transgressing all.

"One who observes this principal commandment observes all the others. He is faithful to me and to his neighbor, and is therefore obedient. He becomes subject to the commandments of the law, for my sake. And with humble patience he endures every labor, and even his neighbor's detraction of him.

"Obedience is of such excellence that you all derive grace from it, just as from disobedience you all derive death. Therefore it is not enough that you should be obedient only in word, and not in practice.

"Obedience is the key that opens heaven, which key my Son placed in the hands of his minister. This minister places it in the hands of everyone who receives holy baptism and promises to renounce the world and all its pomps and delights, and to obey. So everyone has in his own person the very same key that the Word had.

"And if one does not, in the light of faith and with the hand of love, unlock the gate of heaven by means of this key, he never will enter there, in spite of its having been opened by the Word. For though I created you without yourselves, I will not save you without yourselves.

"Therefore you must take the key in your hand and walk by the doctrine of my Word, and not remain seated. That is, you must not place your love in finite things, as do foolish men who follow in Adam's footsteps. Such men cast the key of obedience into the mud of impurity, break it with the hammer of pride, and rust it with self-love.

"This key would have been entirely destroyed had not my only-begotten Son, the Word, come and taken the key of obedience in his hands and purified it in the fire of divine love. For he drew it out of the mud, cleansed it with his blood, straightened it with the knife of justice, and hammered your iniquities into shape on the anvil of his own body. So perfectly did he repair it that no matter how much one may have spoiled his key by his free-will, by the very same free-will, assisted by my grace, he can repair it with the same instruments that were used by my Word.

"Oh! blinder than the blind! Having spoiled the key of obedience, you do not think of mending it! Do you indeed think that the disobedience that closed the door of heaven will open it? Do you think that the pride that fell can rise? Do you think to be admitted to the marriage feast in foul and disordered garments? Do you think that sitting down and binding yourself with the chain of mortal sin, you can walk? or that without a key you can open the door? Do not imagine that you can, for it is a fantastic delusion.

"You must be firm. You must leave mortal sin through holy confession, contrition of heart, atonement, and the heartfelt intention to amend your life. Then you will throw off that hideous and defiled garment and, clothed in the shining nuptial robe, you will hasten, with the key of obedience in your hand, to open the door.

"But bind this key with the cord of self-contempt and hatred of yourself and of the world, and fasten it to the love of pleasing me, your creator. And bind this cord tightly about your waist, for fear you lose it.

"Know, my daughter, there are many who take up this key of obedience, having seen by the light of faith that in no other way can they escape eternal damnation. But they hold it in their hand without wearing this belt, or fastening the key to it with the cord of self-contempt. That is to say that they are not perfectly clothed with my pleasure, but still seek to please themselves. They do not wear the cord of self-contempt, for they do not desire to be despised, but rather take delight in the praise of men.

"Such as these are apt to lose their key. For if they suffer a little extra fatigue, or mental or bodily tribulation, and if, as often happens, the hand of holy desire loosens its grasp, they will lose it. They can indeed find it again if they wish to while they live, but if they do not wish they will never find it. And what will prove to them that they have lost it? Impatience, for patience was united to obedience, and their impatience proves that obedience does not dwell in their soul.

"How sweet and glorious is this virtue of obedience, which contains all the rest, for it is conceived and born of charity. On it is founded the rock of the holy faith. It is a queen whose consort will feel no trouble, but only peace and quiet. The waves of the stormy sea cannot hurt it, nor can any tempest reach the interior of the soul in whom it dwells.

"The obedient one feels no hatred when injured, because he wishes to obey the precept of forgiveness. He does not suffer when his appetites are not satisfied, because obedience has ordered him to desire me alone. For I can and will satisfy all his desires, if he strips himself of worldly riches. And so in all things which would take too long to relate, one who has chosen obedience, the appointed key of heaven, finds peace and quiet. Oh!

"Blessed obedience! You voyage without fatigue, and reach without danger the port of salvation. You are conformed to my only-begotten Son, the Word, so as not to transgress the obedience of the Word, nor abandon his doctrine. You dwell in the love of your neighbor, being anointed with true humility, which saves you from coveting his possessions, contrary to my will.

"You are even cheerful, for your face is never wrinkled with impatience, but it is smooth and pleasant with the happiness of patience. And even in its fortitude you are great by your long endurance, so long that it reaches from earth to heaven and unlocks the celestial door.

"You are a hidden pearl, trampled by the world, abasing yourself, submitting to all creatures. Yet your kingdom is so great that no one can rule you. For you have come out of the mortal servitude of your own sensuality, which destroyed your dignity. And having slain this enemy with hatred and dislike of your own pleasure, you have re-obtained your liberty."

*Here both the misery of the disobedient and the
excellence of the obedient are spoken of.*

"All this, dearest daughter, has been done by my
goodness and providence. For by my providence
the Word repaired the key of obedience.

"But worldly persons, like unbridled horses, without the bit of obedience, go from bad to worse, from
sin to sin, from misery to misery, until they finally
reach the edge of the ditch of death, gnawed by the
worm of their conscience. And though it is true that
they can obey the precepts of the law if they will, and
repent of their disobedience, it is very hard for them
to do so, on account of their long habit of sin.

"Therefore let no one trust in putting off finding
the key of obedience to the moment of his death. For
although everyone may and should hope as long as
he has life, he should not put such trust in this hope
as to delay repentance.

"What is the reason for such blindness that prevents them from recognizing this treasure? The cloud
of self-love and wretched pride, through which
mankind abandoned obedience and fell into disobedience. Being disobedient, they are impatient and in
their impatience they endure intolerable pain. For
impatience has seduced them from the way of Truth,
leading them along a way of lies, making them
slaves and friends of the devils with whom, unless

indeed they amend themselves with patience, they will go to the eternal torments.

"On the contrary, My beloved children, obedient observers of the law, rejoice and exult in My eternal vision with the Immaculate and humble Lamb, the Maker, Fulfiller, and Giver of this law of obedience. Observing this law in this life, they taste peace without any disturbance, and they clothe themselves in the most perfect peace. In peace, they possess every good without any evil, safety without any fear, riches without any poverty, fulfillment without excess, hunger without pain, light without darkness—one supreme infinite good, shared by all those who taste it truly.

"What has placed them in so blessed a state? The blood of the Lamb, by virtue of which the key of obedience has lost its rust, so that, by the virtue of the blood, it has been able to unlock the door.

"Oh! fools and madmen, delay no longer to come out of the mud of impurity, for you seem, like pigs, to wallow in the mire of your own lust. Abandon the injustice, murders, hatreds, rancors, detractions, murmurings, false judgments, and cruelty, with which you treat your neighbors. Abandon your thefts and treacheries, and the disordinate pleasures and delights of the world. Cut off the horns of pride, by which amputation you will extinguish the hatred that is in your heart against your neighbors.

"Compare the injuries that you do to Me and to your neighbor with those done to you, and you will see that those done to you are but trifles. You will see that remaining in hatred you injure Me by transgressing My precept. And you also injure the object of your hate, for you deprive him of your love, whereas you have been commanded to love Me above everything, and your neighbor as yourself.

"No gloss has been put upon these commandments, as if it should have been said, 'If your neighbor injures you do not love him.' Rather, they are to be taken naturally and simply, as they were said to you by My Truth, who Himself literally observed this rule. Literally also should you observe it, and if you do not you will injure your own soul, depriving it of the life of grace.

"Take, oh! take, then, the key of obedience with the light of faith. Do not walk any longer in such darkness or cold, but observe obedience in the fire of love, so that you may taste eternal life together with the other observers of the law."

How the truly obedient receive a hundredfold for one, and also eternal life; and what is meant by this one, and this hundredfold.

"In obedience is fulfilled the saying of the sweet and loving Word, my only-begotten Son, in the Gospel when he replied to Peter's demand, 'Master, we have left everything for your love's sake, and have followed you, what will you give us?' My Truth replied, 'I will give you a hundredfold for one, and you shall possess eternal life.' It is as if my Truth had wished to say, 'You have done well, Peter, for in no other way could you follow me. And I, in this life, will give you a hundredfold for one.' And what is this hundredfold, beloved daughter, besides which the apostle obtained eternal life? To what did my Truth refer? To temporal substance?

"Properly speaking, no. Do I not, however, often cause one who gives alms to multiply in temporal goods? In return for what? In return for the gift of his own will. This is the one, for which I repay him a hundredfold. What is the meaning of the number one hundred? One hundred is a perfect number, and cannot be added to except by recommencing from the first.

"So charity is the most perfect of all the virtues, so perfect that no higher virtue can be attained except by recommencing at the beginning of self-knowledge, and thus increasing many hundredfold in merit. This is that hundredfold that is given to those who have given me the one, that is, their own will, both in general obedience, and in the particular obedience of the religious life.

"And in addition to this hundred you also possess eternal life, for charity alone enters into eternal life, like the mistress of a household bringing with her the fruit of all the other virtues, while the others remain outside. The obedient bring their fruit, I say, into me, the eternal life, in whom they taste eternal life.

"It is not by faith that they taste eternal life, for they experience in its essence that which they have believed through faith. Nor is it by hope, for they possess that for which they had hoped. And so it is with all the other virtues. It is Queen Charity alone who enters and possesses me, her possessor.

"See, therefore, that these little ones receive a hundredfold for one, and also eternal life. For here they receive the fire of divine charity multiplied by one hundred. And because they have received this hundredfold from me, they possess a wonderful and hearty joy. For there is no sadness in charity, but the joy of it makes the heart large and generous, not narrow or double.

"A soul wounded by this sweet arrow does not appear one thing in face and tongue while its heart is different. It does not serve or act towards its neighbor with dissembling and ambition, because charity is an open book to be read by all. Therefore the soul who possesses charity never falls into trouble or the affliction of sadness, or jars with obedience, but remains obedient until death."

*Of the perversities, miseries, and labors of
the disobedient one; and of the miserable
fruits that proceed from disobedience.*

"A wicked, disobedient one dwells in the ship of a religious order with so much pain to himself and others, that in this life he tastes the pledge of hell. He remains always in sadness and confusion of mind, tormented by the sting of conscience, with hatred of his order and his superior, intolerable to himself.

"What a terrible thing it is, my daughter, to see one who has once taken the key of obedience of a religious order, now living in disobedience, to which he has made himself a slave. For of disobedience he has made his master with its companion impatience, nourished by pride and his own pleasure, which pride issues from self-love.

"For him everything is the contrary to what it would be for the obedient man. For how can this wretch be in any other state than suffering, for he is deprived of charity. He is obliged by force to incline the neck of his own will, and pride keeps it erect.

"All his desires are in discord with the will of the order. The order commands obedience, and he loves disobedience. The order commands voluntary poverty, and he avoids it, possessing and acquiring riches. The order commands continence and purity, and he desires lewdness. By transgressing these three vows, my daughter, a religious comes to ruin, and falls into so many miseries, that his aspect is no longer that of a religious but of an incarnate devil.

"I will, however, tell you something of the delusion of such a one, and of the fruit that he obtains by disobedience to the commendation and exhortation of obedience. This wretched man is deluded by his self-love, because the eye of his intellect is fixed, with a dead faith, on pleasing his self-will, and on things of the world. He has left the world in body, but has remained there in his affections. And because obedience seems wearisome to him, he wishes to disobey in order to avoid weariness. Thus he arrives at the greatest weariness of all: For he is obliged to obey either by force or by love, and it would have been better and less wearisome to have obeyed by love than without it.

"Oh! how deluded is such a one, yet no one else deceives him but himself. Wishing to please himself he gives himself only displeasure, for the actions that he will have to do, through the obedience imposed on him, do not please him. He wishes to enjoy delights and make this life his eternity, but the order desires him to be a pilgrim, and continually proves this desire to him. For when he is in a nice, pleasant resting place, where he would like to remain for the pleasures and delights he finds there, he is transferred elsewhere. And the change gives him pain, for his will was active against his obedience. And yet he is obliged to endure the discipline and labors of the order, and thus remains in continual torment.

"See, therefore, how he deludes himself; for, wishing to fly pain, he on the contrary falls into it. For his blindness does not let him know the road of true obedience, so that he walks by the road of lies, believing that he will find delight there, but finding on the contrary pain and bitterness. Who is his guide? Self-love, that is, his own passion for disobedience.

"Like a fool, such a one thinks to navigate this tempestuous sea with the strength of his own arms, trusting in his own miserable knowledge, and will not navigate it in the arms of his order and of his superior. He is indeed in the ship of the order in body, but not in mind.

"Such a man has left his order, in his desire, by not observing the regulations or customs of the order, nor the three vows that he promised to observe at the time of his profession. He swims in the tempestuous sea, tossed to and fro by contrary winds, fastened only to the ship by his clothes, wearing the religious habit on his body but not on his heart.

"Such a one is no friar, but a masquerader, a man only in appearance. His life is lower than an animal's. He does not see that he labors more by swimming with his arms, than the good religious in the ship, or that he is in danger of eternal death. For if his clothes should be suddenly torn from the ship, which will happen at the moment of death, he will have no remedy.

"No, he does not see, for he has darkened his light with the cloud of self-love. And from self-love has come his disobedience, which prevents him seeing his misery; therefore he miserably deceives himself.

"What fruit is produced by this wretched tree? The fruit of death, because the root of his affection is planted in pride, which he has drawn from self-love. Hence everything that issues from this root—flowers, leaves, and fruit—is corrupt, and the three boughs of this tree, which are obedience, poverty, and continence, which spring from the foot of the tree (that is, his affections) are corrupted.

"The leaves produced by this tree, which are his words, are so corrupt that they would be out of place in the mouth of a ribald secular. If he has to preach my doctrine, he does so in polished terms, not simply, as one who should feed souls with the seed of my Word, but with eloquent language.

"Look at the stinking flowers of this tree, which are his various thoughts. These he voluntarily welcomes with delight and pleasure, not fleeing from the occasions of them, but rather seeking them in order to be able to accomplish a sinful act. And the sinful act is the fruit that kills him, depriving him of the light of grace and giving him eternal death.

"What stench comes from this fruit, sprung from the flowers of the tree? The stench of disobedience. For, in the secret place of his heart, he wishes to examine and judge unfaithfully his superior's will. The stench of impurity. For he takes delight in many foul conversations, wretchedly tempting his penitents.

"Wretch that you are, do you not see that under the banner of devotion you conceal a troop of children? This comes from your disobedience. You have not chosen the virtues for your children as does the truly obedient religious. You strive to deceive your superior when you see that he denies you something that your perverse will desires. You use the leaves of smooth or rough words, speaking irreverently and reproving him.

"You can not endure your brother, nor even the smallest word of correction that he may speak to you. In such a case you immediately bring forth the poisoned fruit of anger and hatred against him, judging as done to your hurt, that which was done for your good.

"Why has your brother displeased you? Because you live for your own sensual pleasure. You avoid your cell as if it were a prison, for you have abandoned the cell of self-knowledge, and thus you have fallen into disobedience. That is why you cannot remain in your material cell. You will not appear in the refectory against your will while you have anything to spend; when you have nothing left, necessity takes you there.

"Therefore the obedient have done well, who have chosen to observe their vow of poverty. They have nothing to spend, and therefore they are not led away from the sweet table of the refectory, where obedience nourishes both body and soul in peace and quiet.

"The obedient religious does not think of setting a table, or of providing food for himself like this wretched one, to whose taste it is painful to eat in the refectory, and thus he avoids it. With his lips he approaches me, but with his heart he is far from me.

"The wretched one gladly escapes from the chapter-house when he can through fear of penance. When he is obliged to be there, he is covered with shame and confusion for the faults that he felt no shame to commit.

"What is the cause of this? Disobedience. He does not watch in prayer, and not only does he omit mental prayer, but even the Divine Office to which he is obliged. He has no love for his brother, because he loves no one but himself, and that not with a reasonable but with a bestial love.

"So great are the evils that fall on the disobedient, and so many are the fruits of sorrow that they produce, that the tongue could not relate them.

"Oh! disobedience, which deprives the soul of the light of obedience, destroying peace, and giving war! Disobedience destroys life and gives death. It draws the religious out of the ship of the observance of his order, only to drown him in the sea. It makes him swim in the strength of his own arms and not repose on those of the order.

"Disobedience clothes him with every misery and causes him to die of hunger, taking away from him the food of the merit of obedience. It gives him continual bitterness and deprives him of every sweetness and good. It causes him to dwell with every evil in life and gives him the pledge of cruel torments to endure.

"If this wretched one does not amend his life before his clothes are loosened from the ship at death, disobedience will lead his soul to eternal damnation, together with the devils who fell from heaven, because they rebelled against me. In the same way the disobedient man, having rebelled against obedience and cast away the key that would have opened the door of heaven, opened instead the door of hell with the key of disobedience."

How God does not reward merit according to the labor of the obedient one, nor according to the length of time that it takes, but according to the love and promptness of the truly obedient one; and of the miracles that God has performed by means of this virtue; and of discretion in obedience; and of the works and reward of the truly obedient man.

"I have appointed each of you to labor in the vineyard of obedience in different ways. Every person will receive a wage according to the measure of his love, and not according to the work he does or the length of time for which he works. One who comes early will not have more than one who comes late, as my Truth told you in the holy Gospel through the example of those who were standing idle and were sent by the lord of the vineyard to labor. For he gave the same amount to those who went at dawn as to those who went at six or at nine in the morning. And those who went at noon, at three o'clock, and even at six o'clock, received as much as the first. My Truth showed you in this way that you are rewarded, not according to time or work, but according to the measure of your love.

"Many are placed while in their childhood to work in the vineyard. Some enter later in life, and others in old age. Sometimes these latter labor with such fire of love, seeing the shortness of the time, that they rejoin those who entered in their child-hood, because these have advanced but slowly. By love of obedience, then, does the soul receive its merit, filling the vessel of its heart in me, the Sea of Peace.

"There are many whose obedience is so prompt, and has become so incarnate in them, that not only do they wish to see reason in what is ordered them by their superior, but they hardly wait until the word is out of his mouth. For with the light of faith they understand his intention.

"Therefore the truly obedient one obeys the intention rather than the word, judging that the will of his superior is fixed in my will, and that therefore his command comes from my dispensation, and from my will. That is why I say to you that he obeys the intention rather than the word. He also obeys the word, because he has first spiritually obeyed in affection his superior's will, seeing and judging it by the light of faith to be mine.

"In everything, if you open the eye of the intellect, you will find shown forth the excellence of obedience. Everything else should be abandoned for the sake of this virtue. If you were lifted up in such contemplation and union of mind with me, that your body was raised from the earth, and an obedience were imposed on you, you ought, if possible, to force yourself to arise and fulfill the obedience imposed on you. And you ought to do this, even though one should never leave prayer, except for necessity, charity, or obedience. I say this so that you may see how prompt I wish the obedience of my servants to be, and how pleasing it is to me.

"Everything that the obedient man does is a source of merit to him. If he eats, obedience is his food. If he sleeps, his dreams are obedience. If he walks, if he remains still, if he fasts, if he watches—everything that he does is obedience. If he serves his neighbor, it is obedience that he serves.

"How is he guided in the choir, in the refectory, or his cell? By obedience, with the light of the most holy faith. With this light he has slain and cast from him his humbled self-will, and abandoned himself with self-hatred to the arms of his order and his superior.

"Reposing with obedience in the ship, allowing himself to be guided by his superior, he has navigated the tempestuous sea of this life, with a calm and serene mind and tranquillity of heart, because obedience and faith have taken all darkness from him. He remains strong and firm, having lost all weakness and fear, and having destroyed his own will, from which comes all feebleness and disordinate fear.

"And what is the food of this spouse, obedience? It eats knowledge of self, and of me. It knows its own nonexistence and sinfulness, and knows that I am the One who is, and thus it eats and knows my Truth in the incarnate Word.

"What does it drink? The Blood, in which the Word has shown it my truth and the inexpressible love that I have for it, and the obedience imposed on the Word by me, his eternal Father. So it becomes intoxicated with the love and obedience of the Word. It loses itself and its own opinions and knowledge. And it possesses me by grace and tastes me by love, with the light of faith in holy obedience.

"The obedient one speaks words of peace all his life, and at his death receives what was promised him at his death by his superior. That is, he receives eternal life, the vision of peace, and supreme and eternal tranquillity and rest. This is the inestimable good that no one can value or understand, for, being the infinite good, it cannot be understood by anything smaller than itself. It is like a vessel, which, dipped into the sea, does not comprehend the whole sea, but only the quantity that it contains. The sea alone contains itself.

"So I, the Sea of Peace, am the One who alone can comprehend and value myself truly. In my own estimate and comprehension of myself I rejoice, and this joy, the good that I have in myself, I share with you, and with all, according to the measure of each.

"I do not leave you empty, but fill you, giving you perfect happiness and blessedness. Every person comprehends and knows my goodness in the measure in which it is given to him. Thus, then, the obedient one, ablaze with the light of faith in the truth burning in the furnace of charity, anointed with humility, intoxicated with the Blood, accompanied by his sister patience, and showing self-contempt, fortitude, enduring perseverance, and all the other virtues (that is, with the fruit of the virtues), receives his end from me, his creator."

This is a brief repetition of the entire book.

"I have now, dearest and best beloved daughter, satisfied from the beginning to the end your desire concerning obedience.

"You made four petitions of me with anxious desire, or rather I caused you to make them in order

to increase the fire of my love in your soul. The first
you made for yourself, and I have satisfied it, illu-
minating you with my truth and showing you how
you may know this truth that you desired to know.
And I explained to you how you might come to the
knowledge of the truth through the knowledge of
yourself and me, through the light of faith.

"The second request you made of me was that I
should show mercy to the world.

"In the third you prayed for the mystical body of
the holy church, that I would remove darkness and
persecutions from it, punishing its iniquities in your
person. As to this I explained that no penalty inflicted
in finite time can atone for a sin committed against
me, the infinite Good, unless it is united with the
desire of the soul and contrition of the heart. How
this is done I have explained to you.

"I have also told you that I wish to show mercy
to the world, proving to you that mercy is my special
attribute. For through the mercy and the inestimable
love that I had for mankind, I sent to the earth the
Word, my only-begotten Son. And so that you might
understand things quite clearly, I represented him to
you under the figure of a bridge that reaches from
earth to heaven through the union of my divinity
with your human nature.

"I also showed you, to give you further light
concerning my truth, how this bridge is built on
three steps, namely, on the three powers of the soul.
These three steps I also represented to you, under

figures of your body—the feet, the side, and the mouth, by which I also figured three states of soul— the imperfect state, the perfect state, and the most perfect state, in which the soul arrives at the excellence of unitive love.

"I have shown you clearly in each state the means of cutting away imperfection and reaching perfection. I have shown you how the soul may know by which road it is walking. And I have shown you the hidden delusions of the devil and of spiritual self-love.

"Speaking of these three states I have also spoken of the three judgments that my clemency delivers. The first is in this life. The second is at death; it is on those who die in mortal sin without hope. Of these I told you that they go under the bridge by the devil's road, when I spoke to you of their wretchedness. And the third is that of the last and universal judgment.

"And I told you somewhat of the suffering of the damned and the glory of the blessed, when all shall have reassumed their bodies given by me. And now again I repeat my promise that through the long endurance of my servants I will reform my bride, the church. Therefore I invite you to endure, myself lamenting with you over her iniquities.

"And I have shown you the excellence of the ministers I have given the church, and the reverence in which I wish seculars to hold them. I have shown you the reason their reverence towards my ministers should not diminish on account of the sins of the latter, and how displeasing to me is such lessening of reverence. And I have spoken to you of the virtue of those who live like angels. And while speaking to you on these subjects, I also touched on the excellence of the sacraments.

"And further wishing you to know of the states of tears and whence they proceed, I spoke to you on the subject and told you that all tears issue from the fountain of the heart, and pointed out their causes to you in order. I told you not only of the four states of tears, but also of the fifth, which germinates death.

"I have also answered your fourth request, that I would provide for the particular case of an individual. I have provided, as you know.

"Beyond this, I have explained my providence to you, in general and in particular. I have shown you how everything is made by divine providence, from the first beginning of the world until the end. My providence gives you and permits everything to happen to you, both tribulations and consolations, whether temporal or spiritual.

"Divine providence grants every circumstance of your life for your good, in order that you may be sanctified in me, and that my truth may be fulfilled in you. That truth is that I created you in order to possess eternal life, and manifested this with the blood of my only-begotten Son, the Word.

"I have also fulfilled your desire and my promise to speak of the perfection of obedience and the imperfection of disobedience. And I have shown you how obedience can be obtained and how it can be destroyed. I have shown it to you as a universal key, and so it is.

"I have also spoken to you of particular obedience, and of the perfect and imperfect, and of those in religion, and of those in the world, explaining the condition of each distinctly to you. I have spoken to you of the peace given by obedience, and the war of disobedience. I have told you how the disobedient man is deceived, showing you how death came into the world by the disobedience of Adam.

"Now I, the eternal Father, the supreme and eternal Truth, give you this conclusion of the whole matter: In the obedience of the only-begotten Word, my Son, you have life, and just as from that first Old Man you contracted the infection of death, so all of you who are willing to take the key of obedience have contracted the infection of the life of the New Man, sweet Jesus, of whom I made a bridge because the road to heaven was broken.

"And now I urge you and my other servants to grieve, for by your grief and humble and continual prayer I will show mercy to the world. Die to the world and hasten along this way of truth, so as not to be taken prisoner if you go slowly. I demand this of you now more than at first, for now I have manifested to you my truth.

"Beware that you never leave the cell of self-knowledge, but in this cell preserve and spend the treasure that I have given you, which is the doctrine of truth founded upon the living stone, sweet Christ Jesus, clothed in light which scatters darkness. With this doctrine clothe yourself, my best beloved and sweetest daughter, in the truth."

How this most devout servant of God, thanking and praising God, makes prayer for the whole world and for the holy church, and, commending the virtue of faith, brings this work to an end.

Then that servant of God, having seen with the eye of the intellect, and having known, by the light of holy faith, the truth and excellence of obedience, hearing and tasting it with love and ecstatic desire, gazed upon God's divine majesty and gave thanks to him in these words:

"Thanks, thanks to you, eternal Father, for you have not despised me, the work of your hands, nor turned your face from me, nor despised my desires. You, the Light, have not regarded my darkness. You, true Life, have not regarded my living death. You, the Physician, have not been repelled by my grave infirmities. You, the eternal Purity, have not considered the many miseries of which I am full. You, who are the Infinite, have overlooked that I am finite. You, who are Wisdom, have overlooked my folly. Your wisdom, your goodness, your clemency, your infinite good, have overlooked these infinite evils and sins, and the many others that are in me.

"Having known the truth through your clemency, I have found your charity and the love of my neighbor. What has constrained me? Not my virtues, but only your charity.

"May that same charity constrain you to illuminate the eye of my intellect with the light of faith, so that I may know and understand the truth that you have manifested to me. Grant that my memory may be capable of retaining your benefits. Grant that my will may burn in the fire of your charity. Grant that that fire may so work in me that I may give my body even to the shedding of blood. Grant that by that blood given for love of the Blood, together with the key of obedience, I may unlock the door of heaven. I ask this of you with all my heart, for every rational creature, both in general and in particular, in the mystical body of the holy church.

"I confess and do not deny that you loved me before I existed, and that your love for me is inexpressible, as if you were mad with love for your creature. Oh, eternal Trinity! Oh, Godhead, which gave value to the blood of your Son! You, eternal Trinity, are a deep Sea, into which the deeper I plunge the more I find, and the more I find the more I seek. The soul cannot be filled to excess in your abyss, for it continually hungers after you, the eternal Trinity, desiring to see you with light in your light.

"As the deer desires the spring of living water, so my soul desires to leave the prison of this dark body and see you in truth. How long, eternal Trinity, fire and abyss of love, will your face be hidden from my eyes? Melt at once the cloud of my body. The knowledge that you have given me of yourself in your truth, constrains me to long to abandon the heaviness of my body, and to give my life for the glory and praise of your name.

"For I have tasted and seen, with the light of the intellect in your light, the abyss of you, the eternal Trinity. And I have seen the beauty of your human creature. For, looking at myself in you, I saw myself to be your image, my life being given me by your power, eternal Father. And I saw your wisdom, which belongs to your only-begotten Son, shining in my intellect and my will, and being one with your Holy Spirit, who proceeds from you and your Son, by whom I am able to love you.

"You, eternal Trinity, are my creator, and I am the work of your hands. And I know, through the new creation that you have given me in the blood of your Son, that you are enamored of the beauty of your workmanship.

"Oh, abyss! Oh, eternal Godhead! Oh, deep Sea! What more could you give me than yourself? You are the fire that ever burns without being consumed; in your heat you consume all the soul's self-love. You are the fire that takes away all cold. With your light you illuminate me so that I may know all your truth. You are the light above all light, which illuminates supernaturally the eye of my intellect, and clarifies the light of faith so abundantly and so perfectly, that I see that my soul is alive, and that in this light it receives you, the true light.

"By the light of faith I have acquired wisdom in the Word—your only-begotten Son. In the light of faith I am strong, constant, and persevering. In the light of faith I hope; do not let me faint by the way.

"This light, without which I would still walk in darkness, teaches me the road. And for this I said, eternal Father, that you have illuminated me with the light of holy faith.

"Of a truth this light is a sea, for the soul revels in you, eternal Trinity, the Sea of Peace. The water of the sea is not turbid, and causes no fear to the soul, for the soul knows the truth: It is a deep that manifests sweet secrets, so that where the light of your faith abounds, the soul is certain of what it believes.

"This water is a supernatural mirror into which you, the eternal Trinity, bid me gaze. You hold it with the hand of love, so that I may see myself, who am your creature. There I am represented in you, and you are represented in me, through the union that you made of your Godhead with our humanity.

"For this light I know represents you to me: You, the supreme and infinite good, blessed and incomprehensible good, inestimable good, beauty above all beauty, wisdom above all wisdom—for you are wisdom itself.

"You, the food of the angels, have given yourself in a fire of love to mankind. You, the garment that covers all our nakedness, feed the hungry with your sweetness.

"Sweet, without any bitterness! Eternal Trinity! In your light, which you have given me with the light of holy faith, I have known the many and wonderful things you have declared to me. You have explained to me the path of supreme perfection, so that I may no longer serve you in darkness, but with light. And you have shown me how I may be the mirror of a good and holy life, and arise from my miserable sins.

"Through my sins I have served you in darkness until now. I have not known your truth and have not loved it. Why did I not know you? Because I did not see you with the glorious light of the holy faith. And because the cloud of self-love darkened the eye of my intellect. But you, the eternal Trinity, have dissipated the darkness with your light.

"Who can attain to your greatness, and give you thanks for such immeasurable gifts and benefits as you have given me in this doctrine of truth? For this doctrine has been a special grace over and above the ordinary graces that you give to your other creatures.

"You have been willing to condescend to my need and to that of your creatures—the need to examine the thoughts and feelings of our heart. Having first given me the grace to ask the question, you reply to it, and satisfy your servant, penetrating me with a ray of grace, so that in that light I may give you thanks.

"Clothe me, clothe me with yourself, eternal Truth, so that I may run my mortal course with true obedience and the light of holy faith. For with that light I feel that my soul is about to become intoxicated afresh."